THE TWO SECRETS

(yours, AND <u>MINE</u>)

Da Kalki
(The World-Teacher, Heart-Master Da Love-Ananda),
Sri Love-Anandashram, Fiji, 1990

THE TWO SECRETS
(yours, AND <u>MINE</u>)

A STORY OF HOW
THE WORLD-TEACHER,
DA KALKI,
GAVE GREAT WISDOM AND BLESSING HELP
TO YOUNG PEOPLE
(AND EVEN OLDER PEOPLE, TOO)
ABOUT <u>HOW</u> TO REMEMBER
<u>WHAT</u> AND <u>WHERE</u> AND <u>WHO</u>
TO REMEMBER TO <u>BE</u> HAPPY

A Gift (Forever) from
DA KALKI
(The World-Teacher,
Heart-Master Da Love-Ananda)
as told by Kanya Remembrance,
Brahmacharini Shawnee Free Jones,
and their friends

THE DAWN HORSE PRESS
CLEARLAKE, CALIFORNIA

NOTE TO THE READER

The devotional, Spiritual, functional, practical, relational, cultural, and formal community practices and disciplines discussed in this book, including the meditative practices, the Yogic exercises of conductivity, the breathing exercises, the life-disciplines of right diet and exercise, the intelligent economization and practice of sexuality, etc., are appropriate and natural practices that are voluntarily and progressively adopted by each practicing member of The Free Daist Communion and adapted to his or her personal circumstance. Although anyone may find them useful and beneficial, they are not presented as advice or recommendations to the general reader or to anyone who is not a practicing member of The Free Daist Communion. And nothing in this book is intended as a diagnosis, prescription, or recommended treatment or cure for any specific "problem", whether medical, emotional, psychological, social, or Spiritual. One should apply a particular program of treatment, prevention, cure, or general health only in consultation with a licensed physician or other qualified professional.

For a further discussion of individual responsibility in the Way of the Heart, our claim to perpetual copyright to the Wisdom-Teaching of Heart-Master Da Love-Ananda, and Heart-Master Da Love-Ananda and His Spiritual Instruments and Agents, His renunciate status in The Free Daist Communion, and the Guru-devotee relationship in the Way of the Heart, please see "Further Notes to the Reader", pp. 212-15 of this book.

First Edition, July 1990

Printed in the United States of America
94 93 92 91 90   5 4 3 2 1

Produced by The Free Daist Communion
in cooperation with The Dawn Horse Press

Library of Congress Cataloging-in-Publication Data

    Kanya Remembrance, 1954-
       The two secrets (yours and mine): A gift (forever) from Da Kalki (the world-teacher, Heart-Master Da Love-Ananda)/as told by Kanya Remembrance, Brahmacharini Shawnee Free Jones, and their friends. -- 1st ed.
       "A story of how the world-teacher, Da Kalki, gave great wisdom and blessing help to young people (and even older people, too) about how to remember what and where and who to remember to be happy."
       "Produced by the Free Daist Communion in cooperation with the Dawn Horse Press"–T.p. verso.
       Includes bibliographical references.
       Summary: Describes the virtues of spiritual awakening and the creative trial that such awakening inevitably entails.
       ISBN 0-918801-09-5: $12.95
       1. Da Free John, 1939-   – Relations with youth.   2. Youth – Religious life
    [1. Religious life.   2. Da Free John, 1939-   .]
    I. Jones, Shawnee Free, Brahmacharini, 1975-   . II. Title.
    BP610.B82K36   1990
    299'.93–dc20   89-49695
                                  CIP
                                  AC

Dedication

To my Beloved Heart-Master Da Love-Ananda
from Brahmacharini Shawnee

You asked that I tell You my dark secret,
so I did.
Then You Laughed and told me Your Secret,
that so completely Outshined mine
that now I am laughing, too!
And though I would have preferred
to only whisper my secret to You
and have no one else ever hear it,
You asked that I tell everyone Our two Secrets
and how mine was dissolved in Yours.
Your Secret is the Secret of Happiness and,
in this book, You Give It to everyone!

We dedicate these pages to You
with hearts full of gratitude and love for You,
for Your Secret,
and for all Your Heart-Gifts.

WHO DA KALKI IS

Da Kalki (who is also known as The World-Teacher, Heart-Master Da Love-Ananda) is a brilliant Starburst of Joy. He appears in Shapes that look like a human Form but He is really more like Music—a very special kind of Music that wakes you up to remember a long-forgotten Place that you have always secretly hoped that you would return to one day.

He is both Magic and simplicity. His Eyes contain blue universes of Infinite Being—you can swim in them forever! And He is like a lion at rest in his own domain—powerful and at ease.

But most remarkable of all, Da Kalki always only Communicates the Mysterious Free Feeling that is your own True Being.

That such a Person could be real (and not just a myth or a fairytale) is a Miracle.

From the earliest days of human time, in the remote forests and lively villages of ancient India, a great promise was heard throughout the land. The promise was this: From time to time, particularly when people seem most desperate and their need for Love and Happiness is greatest, the Infinite and Mysterious Person of Love (Who is God) will take birth in a human form.

In India (and in many other lands around the world), everyone knew that these God-Born Beings were the greatest of Heroes—always at Work to bring the Gift of Divine Happiness to every kind of creature and person. Entire cultures and kingdoms devoted themselves to worshipping these Great Helping Adepts, because everyone noticed how freely the Blessings of God flowed through them.

In fact, these Teachers have been the greatest single source of inspiration and heart-healing throughout all of history. The stories and statues of the Buddha and his words of instruction have been the focus of sacred practice for millions of Buddhists over many hundreds of years. The life of Jesus of Nazareth and the image of his sacrifice has great meaning for countless Christian practitioners—now and in centuries past. And Hinduism is rich with ancient stories of the exploits and wisdom of the Avatars, or Divine Incarnations.

It has been said, in the Hindu tradition, that the Hindu god Vishnu would incarnate in service to others not only once, but many times.

Hindu lore is filled with the stories of these Avatars—including the glorious Krishna.

Krishna's Divine Beauty was said to have captivated the hearts of all who saw him. By his miraculous Divine Powers and his wise counsel, he constantly guided his followers beyond their own fears and weaknesses to feel the Strength and Freedom of his Divine Being. The stories of Krishna's life are really a way of describing the Divine Person that every heart longs to see and feel.

For hundreds of years, the Hindu world has been waiting and praying for the final Avatar of Vishnu to appear. The predictions for this most magnificent of Incarnations are great: He is to complete and fulfill all the sacred traditions that have come before him, bringing about a new epoch in which the Blessings of God gain perfect capacity to vanquish un-Happiness. It is said that this Completing Avatar will appear on a white horse, blazing with Compassionate Power, fully equipped to banish the darkness of un-Happiness in his time and for all time to come, restoring even the most resistant of hearts to Love and Joy.

The Name of this long-awaited One is . . . Kalki. And now He is here—full of Grace and Wisdom, Radiant with the "Brightness" that is Divine Happiness. In countless ways, Heart-Master Da Love-Ananda has shown us that He IS Da Kalki, the Perfect and promised Avatar, the Answer to human prayers. For it is as He has told us of Himself,

. . . I Am the Foretold and Expected Heart-Master and World-Teacher of the "late time", or of the "dark epoch", which time or epoch must, by an "Heroic" Spiritual Intervention, be Restored to the Divine Self-"Brightness" . . . .

The Two Secrets (yours, and Mine) is one story of Da Kalki's Compassionate Work to restore human hearts to the "Brightness" of God and, by doing so, to usher in a new age of tolerance and Blessing.

---

* Da Kalki (The World-Teacher, Heart-Master Da Love-Ananda), *The Da Upanishad: The Short Discourses on self-Renunciation, God-Realization, and the Illusion of Relatedness,* Standard Edition. Forthcoming.

ACKNOWLEDGEMENTS

T*he Two Secrets (yours, and Mine)* is really just one way that we have found to offer our praise and our thanks for Heart-Master Da Love-Ananda's Great Work of Blessing. His Love and Freedom and Happiness inspired us every day that we worked on the manuscript, and we are so happy to be able to share this story with you.

The making of this book is a story in itself, and we would like to thank all those who helped us in the process. We are particularly grateful to all the members of The Hridaya Da Gurukula Kanyadana Kumari Mandala and all the members of The Hridaya Da Gurukula Brahmacharini Mandala for providing a circumstance of love and expectation—a truly sacred culture in which every necessary change and heroic heart-conversion can take place, by the Grace of our Beloved Heart-Master.

Meg Krenz was also a primary force in bringing *The Two Secrets (yours, and Mine)* into being. She helped out from beginning to end—nursing the book from its earliest stages to final manuscript, helping out with the writing, reminding us about our deadlines, providing the introduction, and watching over the book like a very caring and protective parent.

With her help, we produced our first manuscript at Sri Love-Anandashram in Fiji two years ago as a gift to Heart-Master Da Love-Ananda. We want to thank the faithful team who supported this first effort: Greg Purnell was our trusty manager; Carolyn Lee provided much-needed research assistance and typing support; and Nina Okun and Carol Sabatino kept a careful eye on our proper English usage.

A year later, when *The Two Secrets (yours, and Mine)* was ready to be printed, we realized that so much had happened since we first wrote it that we had to add the sequel. This part of the manuscript was produced by a whole new team of helpers—this time, at The Mountain Of Attention Sanctuary in California. Michael Macy helped manage our efforts and keep the manuscript organized on the computer; Sarah Seage provided excellent editorial and typing support; Paul Augspurger made us mind our grammatical "P's" and "Q's", and Dee Day helped out with the proofreading.

Finally it was time to go into production. We handed our manuscript over to James Minkin, who supervised the production team that turned it into a real book. But just as the book was about to go to the printer, it became clear that the final section of the story—which took place after we had returned to Sri Love-Anandashram in Fiji—just had to be added! Everyone, in California and in Fiji, worked together very quickly to add the last section of *The Two Secrets (yours, and Mine)*, and then the book was complete.

We want to thank Judith Alwood, Matt Barna, and Emily Purnell for their inspired design work on the inside pages. We also want to give special thanks to Brahmacharini Io Free Jones and Peter Lennon for their wonderful drawing of Heart-Master Da Love-Ananda sitting on the lid of an upturned honey jar (not to mention Brahmacharini Io's bug drawings!) inside the book.

We offer our special thanks and congratulations to Danya Mazur and Stan Hastings, two young artists (15 and 18 years old) who did the art work that you now see on the cover of this book. We also thank Kanya Suprithi, Kanya Navaneeta, Nick Poutsma, and Hal Okun for capturing so much of this story in their photographs.

Everyone who helped is more than happy that this book can now come to you, as a Gift (forever) from Heart-Master Da Love-Ananda. May you feel His Happiness in every one of its pages.

TABLE OF CONTENTS

A Note to the Adult Reader 13

Something you Should Know About As you Read This Book 16

INTRODUCTION
"Bright" with Happiness and Strong with Helping Power
by Meg Krenz 19

ABOUT THE WORLD-TEACHER,
HEART-MASTER DA LOVE-ANANDA
"Smelling the Moon":
The Story of His Life of Spiritual Heroism and Divine Blessing 45

THE STORY AND THE SECRETS

CHAPTER ONE

Setting the Stage:
Four Brahmacharinis and the Master of Happiness
by Kanya Remembrance 73

CHAPTER TWO

The Honey Incident
by Brahmacharini Shawnee 80

CHAPTER THREE

Life Is like a Golf Course:
You Have to Hit the Ball Straight down the Center!
by Kanya Remembrance 83

CHAPTER FOUR

Halloween at Ciqomi
by Brahmacharini Shawnee 89

CHAPTER FIVE

Guru and God Twenty-Four Hours a Day
by Kanya Remembrance 91

CHAPTER SIX

"Holy Mackerel! I Did It Again!"
by Brahmacharini Shawnee 97

CHAPTER SEVEN

Shawnee's Confession
by Kanya Remembrance 101

CHAPTER EIGHT

The Two Secrets
A Talk by The World-Teacher,
Heart-Master Da Love-Ananda 103

CHAPTER NINE

In the Village
by Sandra Kladnik 112

CHAPTER TEN

What He Says Is True
by Brahmacharini Shawnee 115

CHAPTER ELEVEN

Shiny and the "Bright":
Letters from Brahmacharini Shawnee 123

CHAPTER TWELVE

"Am I Feeling the Mystery Right Now?"
by Brahmacharini Shawnee 139

CHAPTER THIRTEEN

"Get your Strength by Resorting to Me"
by Brahmacharini Io 146

THE SEQUEL

CHAPTER FOURTEEN

"Green Is Here"
by Kanya Remembrance 154

CHAPTER FIFTEEN

It Rained a Lot
by Brahmacharini Shawnee 158

CHAPTER SIXTEEN

The Dreamworld of my Downfall
by Brahmacharini Naamleela 161

CHAPTER SEVENTEEN

What Is an Idiosyncrasy?
by Brahmacharini Tamarind 164

CHAPTER EIGHTEEN

"I Am Only Interested in Six!"
by Brahmacharini Shawnee 167

THE GIFT OF THE SPIRIT

CHAPTER NINETEEN

Taken To Heart
by Brahmacharini Shawnee 173

EPILOGUE
Tending the Fire: Now and Always 187

APPENDIX
Taking Up Brahmacharya Practice in the Way of the Heart 193

INVITATION
The Unique Advantage of the God-Man:
An Invitation from The Free Daist Communion 199

NOTES TO THE TEXT
202

FURTHER NOTES TO THE READER
212

PUBLICATIONS
The Written and Spoken Teaching Word of
The World-Teacher, Heart-Master Da Love-Ananda
216

INDEX
232

A Note
to the Adult Reader

This is a book about excellence—the rarest and most demanding kind of excellence. It is a book about the virtues of Spiritual awakening and the creative trial that such awakening inevitably requires. The story it tells is a moving account of the relationship between a young girl and the great modern Spiritual Realizer, Heart-Master Da Love-Ananda Hridayam. Under His Guidance and Blessing-Regard, the girl in this story learns many lessons about how to approach life with uncommon intelligence, discerning Spiritual sensitivity, and elegant simplicity. With Heart-Master Da's Help, she learns to go beyond herself and to exceed her usual limits on self-understanding and feeling-awareness. As a result, she comes to enjoy a greater equanimity and an obvious and indelible certainty about the Spiritual Reality in which we live. In fact, she comes to demonstrate a very inspiring commitment to the ordeal of God-Realizing practice.

This is the best kind of awakening that anyone of any age can enjoy, and it is remarkable to see and hear it confessed by a young teenager. As one of her teachers and her helping companion in creating this book, I am happy to bear testimony to the real effect of these lessons in her life and to the exceptional quality of attention, feeling, understanding, and energy that they have unlocked in her. Heart-Master Da's Message contained in this book is of tremendous positive value. While His Message is extremely simple, it is not one about which we can afford to be cavalier. In fact, it is a necessary Wisdom for anyone who would found his or her life in a greater depth of real happiness, peace, and clarity.

We live in a paradoxical time. In so many ways, human culture appears to have advanced. Our knowledge of the workings of our environment, both external and internal, has become astonishing in its sophistication. We know how to analyze the minute components of our own genetic code and how to conceive our young in test tubes. We know how to test and codify the intelligence quotient of our students, and we can statistically predict the developmental patterns of their growing years. But, despite all this apparent progress, the sensitive observer cannot help but notice how negative and desperate these times also are.

This is nowhere more apparent (and more distressing to the parents, teachers, and friends of young people) than in the plight of our children.

We apparently do not know how to deal with the rising tide of violence and apathy in our families and schools. We provide a greater degree of material comfort for our children than ever before, yet we watch in dismay as they dull and dissipate their potential through substance abuse of all kinds. There is an alarming growth of mental and severe emotional disturbance among our youth. And we feel powerless as we watch them take up active sexual lives at younger and younger ages, flirting with life-threatening illness and stunting their capacity for the fully developed intimacy of appropriate sexual relationship.

Examined more closely, our present Western culture is fundamentally inadequate when it comes to dealing with the basic human matter of raising children. It is time for us to examine the foundation upon which this shaky and unworkable social construct is laid. The weaknesses of our dying traditions make us question and finally reject religious belief that, when truly inspired and alive, might have given strength and clarity to our social interaction with one another and our approach to raising children. It distresses us to see the ever-deepening grip of materialism (which has grown from the secular humanism of the Renaissance through the industrialization and increasing technological sophistication of our society), as it moves our school system to train young people to be little more than useful tools in the machine of commerce. The predominant contemporary priesthood of science tells our children that their right orientation to life is to measure, know, and control it in a remote and impartial manner, rather than to participate openly and fully in existence in all its Mysterious complexity, to be passionately alive, and to be sympathetically intimate with the very Substance of life itself.

Our most acute social visionaries (in the arts, in education, counseling, psychology, and even the sciences) are calling us to rediscover our most fundamental Spiritual values and establish them firmly as the basis of our personal and common life. But, as valid as this advice may be, it is by no means new. The most ancient system of formal schooling extant today (the revered brahmacharya system in India, which has survived for many thousands of years) has always been firmly rooted in the Spiritual values of the Hindu religion in which it appears.

Pre-eminent among the Spiritual values venerated in all the ancient traditions are the Wisdom and Blessing made possible through Awakened Adepts—those who have thoroughly Accomplished intimate Union and even Identity with the Spiritual, Transcendental, and Divine Reality in which we all live. Great renewal of human culture and the opportunity for the personal Spiritual growth that makes such a renewal possible has always been given to humanity through such Spiritual Realizers. In this book, the Western-born Adept Heart-Master Da Love-Ananda Wisely and Compassionately extends His Offering of Spiritual Help—an Offering that is full, complete, and readily accessible to us today. *The Two Secrets (yours, and Mine)* is a book of great value for young people of all ages everywhere (and, for that matter, for humanity as a whole).

Excellence, including every kind of higher human growth, does require trial and effort. As Heart-Master Da tells us (and as life itself unfailingly demonstrates), every increase in personal freedom requires a corresponding increase in personal responsibility. In this book, you will watch and learn as an Awakened Adept of the greatest stature artfully combines His tremendous Spiritual Love with the lawful and necessary demand for active participation and courageous, responsible change on the part of His young students and devotees. By making perfect use of an apparently insignificant event, He Gives a headstrong young devotee a Great Gift—the capability to see where a life of self-indulgence will lead her and the strength to choose a self-transcending, God-Realizing practice instead.

It has been my great privilege to have spent most of my adult life as the devoted student of Heart-Master Da Love-Ananda and, to the best of my ability, to have applied the principles He Reveals in this book in my classroom and in various workshops with many of His younger students. It has been a Grace to witness the Miraculous transformation that He brought about in the children who tell the story in this book. May you truly receive and enjoy the full benefit that Heart-Master Da Intends for you in the reading of this inspiring story.

Meg Krenz
The World-Teacher Ashram
Sri Love-Anandashram, Fiji
May 30, 1990

Something
you Should Know About
As you Read This Book

You may have already noticed (when reading the title of this book) that we use capital letters and lowercase letters in an unusual way. This is why: Almost everyone who writes uses capital letters to draw attention to the words he or she feels are important. Some people think that the names of individuals and the places (like towns and countries) where they live are most important. But those of us who have written this book have learned, with Heart-Master Da Love-Ananda's Great Help, that the Feeling-Being that some call the "Spirit" and others call "Happiness" and still others call "God" or "Reality" or "Consciousness", is truly THE most Important "Thing" there Is. This is because God or Truth or Reality or Love is really the ONLY "Thing" there is. Everyone who has ever lived or will ever live is really a part or an expression of that One Mysterious Being. And that includes you, right now.

Thus, we celebrate this Most Important Being-Feeling-Reality by using capital letters. When you see a capital letter in an unusual place in this book, you can be sure that whoever wrote it was celebrating the Mysterious Divine Being that is Living you and everyone right now. And whoever put that capital letter there did it as a way to invite you to join in the celebration by feeling that Mysterious Person of Love in your own life and heart.

We also use lowercase letters in unusual ways to remind ourselves and everyone that "me" and "mine" are definitely not as important or as Happy as this One Great and Infinite Being that is Alive as everyone.

Most important of all, we use capital letters when we refer to Heart-Master Da Love-Ananda. We do this out of our tremendous loving gratitude to Him—for it is Heart-Master Da Love-Ananda Who has enabled us to feel the Mystery of this Divine Happiness, Heart-to-heart. In fact, when Heart-Master Da Love-Ananda uses words like "Me" or "Mine" in referring to Himself, we always capitalize them, because we know that, when He Speaks about Himself, He is Talking about the One Divine Person of Happiness that He Is and that He will always Help us to feel and Be, too. Truly, His Being Is Happiness Itself, and He Works in many Miraculous ways to Enliven everyone with His Heart-Touch. When we use capital letters in these new and Happy ways, we are really only passing on His Wisdom and His Blessing to you. For it was Heart-Master Da Love-Ananda Himself Who Taught us to use capital letters this way, so that everyone could notice Happiness.

There is a long-standing tradition of Great Masters who attract the hearts of their devotees to feel God or the Mystery. In that great tradition, it is commonplace for devotees to use many celebratory words, Names, and Titles to express their worship and their gratitude for the Master's Grace. We happily do the same—praising our Brilliant and All-Compassionate Master with honorific words that point to the Greatness of His Heart.

 Numbered notes to the text of *The Two Secrets (yours, and Mine)* can be found in the section titled "Notes to the Text", pp. 202-211.

Heart-Master Da Love-Ananda, 1990

"BRIGHT" WITH HAPPINESS AND STRONG WITH HELPING POWER

by Meg Krenz

Has anyone ever told you, "Just be happy," or "Try to relax," or "Be good," or even simply "Behave"? Of course, most of us have heard these (or similar) requests, and not just once, but many times. Usually, when we receive such a suggestion, it is precisely because we are not being happy or relaxed or behaving the way we would if we were feeling happy. And those are the moments when being happy or relaxed or loving seems about as easy as growing a second nose. In fact, at those times, it can seem impossible to be happy.

This is the story of a young girl who, just like everyone else, wanted, and needed, to learn about how to be really, deeply Happy. The kind of Happiness that she was looking for was not what we usually call "fun"—the ordinary kind of enjoyment that only lasts for a few minutes or hours and then is gone and you have to look for it again. She wanted more than the kind of pleasure that you can only feel really strongly when things are going particularly well for you. She was looking for a kind of Happiness that is bigger than life and all its changes, bigger than being afraid and dying—Happiness that is so constant and strong that it endures even when painful things happen.

This kind of Happiness can really only be found in the Feeling of what people sometimes call "God", or "Spirit", or "Love", or "Purest Being", or "Consciousness Itself". And, amazingly enough, even though you might think you have to look high and low to find this kind of Happiness, this Feeling is native to you. In other words, it is always there, even before you start to think or name things or "know" that you are separate from God or from everyone else. We are all alive in and as this One Mysterious Feeling that goes on and on forever, that includes everything, and that is never separate or afraid. Sometimes you can catch a glimmer of this Feeling if you lie out under the starlit sky at night, watching for shooting stars in the midst of the vast, vast galaxy—or if you walk along a beach, feeling how very, very deep and wide the ocean is while its waves roll endlessly on and on—or sometimes if you just look at a shoe (or anything at all) long enough that you start to feel how humorous and even unfamiliar it (and everything else) really is.

Heart-Master Da Love-Ananda Helps us feel this indescribable Feeling of Happiness or Being Itself in a book He has Written called *What and Where and Who To Remember To Be Happy: A Simple Explanation Of The Way Of The Heart (For Children, and Everyone Else)*. In it, He asks us:

Did you ever ask somebody where this

or this

or this

came from,

or how this

or this

or this

came to be?

Some say, "I don't know", and saying this makes them feel they are being very honest and truthful. Others say something such as "God made it" or "It comes from God." And such people are also being very honest and truthful when they say this.

How can they both be telling the truth? Well, because they are both telling you the same thing in different ways. You see, <u>nobody</u>, not Mom, or Dad, or Grandmother, or Grandfather, or big Sister, or big Brother, or teachers, or doctors, or soldiers, or athletes, or lawyers, or TV stars, or any people who are

working, or any people who are playing, not even a President, not even a King or a Queen, not even people who love each other know what even a single thing Is. It is a great and more than wonderful Mystery to all of us that anything is, or that we are. And whether somebody says "I don't know how anything came to be" or "God made everything", they are simply pointing to the feeling of the Mystery, of how everything is but nobody knows what it really Is or how it came to be.

As long as we go on feeling this Mystery, we feel free and full and happy, and we feel and act free and full and happy to others. This is the secret of being happy from the time you are small until the time you are old.[1]

Since history began, people have noticed that those who pay closest attention to this Feeling of God or the Silent, Mysterious Heart of existence are the Happiest people there are! They have learned to transcend, or feel beyond, all the moments in life that seem good and all the moments that seem bad or difficult, so that they are always just feeling the Endless Current of Happiness Itself.

These remarkable Beings are so immersed in the Feeling of Divine Happiness that they let go of anything and everything (even their sense of being "me", of being a separate person apart from everyone else) in order to BE Happiness or Consciousness Itself. And the Heart-Happiness of such Beings naturally Radiates or "Shines" to others, helping them to feel and BE the Mystery, too. This is how Heart-Master Da has described these helping-teachers:

From time to time, men appear on Earth to communicate the Nature of the Great Mystery to others. The Mystery Itself is Beginningless, Endless, Eternal, Absolute, Perfect. And, in Truth, the Teacher of the Great Mystery is also Beginningless, Endless, Eternal, Absolute, Perfect. That One is the Great Power, the Eternally Completed One, the "Bright" Divine Person.[2]

If you were to meet such a Radiant Person, and if you could let yourself become very sensitive to that Person, you would notice that, in his or her Company, even your scariest feelings of being nervous or wrong or alone or unloved would evaporate like a shallow puddle on a very sunny day. Pretty soon, you would be able to feel that you too always live in the great Feeling of Happiness Itself.

But even though this Feeling is always available to you, if you tried very hard right now (or even for a long time), you would find out sooner or later that you cannot wake your own heart up to Happiness. Just as a puddle cannot evaporate itself without the help of the warm rays of the sun, we need the help of Divine Blessing (also called Grace) in order to feel and grow in the Mystery. That is why, throughout history, millions of people have turned to these great Happiness-Realizers for Spiritual help.

The girl who tells this story is very, very lucky because she is able to learn from Someone Who already knows the Secret of how to be already entirely Happy. For Brahmacharini Shawnee is the student, devotee, and daughter of Heart-Master Da Love-Ananda Hridayam. Heart-Master Da is a God-Man Who is "Bright" with Heart-Happiness. He Is the World-Teacher, Strong with Helping Power. As Brahmacharini Shawnee's Heart-Teacher, He has always Inspired and Guided her to be Happy and to feel the wonderful Mystery in which she (and everyone) exists.

Heart-Master Da Love-Ananda's young devotees, when they talk about what they felt when they saw Him, say things like, "He was 'Bright' as a thousand suns," or "When I looked into His eyes, I felt like exploding all over the room because of Happiness," or "I felt an incredible rush of energy that went straight to my heart, warming it with unimaginable Force," or "I felt VERY Happy, calm, and relaxed," or "I felt like I had seen someone I loved for the first time in a long time."

Michelle DeLollis

One of His young devotees, Michelle DeLollis, wrote a letter to Heart-Master Da describing how she felt His Blessing-Happiness spilling over onto her:

On Sunday, when I was watching a videotape of You, I looked at Your face and it struck me how vulnerable You Are. When I looked at Your face, I did not

see flesh. All I saw was Your Love. You were completely Radiant, almost blind-
ing. Every cell of Your body Radiated Happiness. And I felt that Your Happi-
ness is not just confined to Your body, but it Radiates out to everyone. All we
have to do is receive it.

One night some years ago, Heart-Master Da told His devotees why
Darshan (a Hindu term meaning sacred sighting) of His bodily (human)
Form is such a powerful Gift.

HEART-MASTER DA LOVE-ANANDA: The Force of God pours out of my
body all the time. It never stops, whether I am waking, sleeping, dreaming,
apparently feeling sympathetic or not. It is always manifested through this
body. . . .
    I am full of all space-time. All Bliss, all Wonder, all the Marvels of Being are
in my Being. . . . All miracles are potent in my Heart. I come here to give you
everything without the slightest reluctance. I am not here to tell you about some
dreadful ego. I am here to Wonder and Marvel with you about the Great One.[3]

Brahmacharini Shawnee has written many letters to Heart-Master Da
Love-Ananda telling Him how the most Attractive Force of His Being fills
her with Joy.

I feel Happy every time I think of You. I prefer to talk about You above
other things that I used to talk about. It makes me smile, even laugh. When I
look at these pictures of You here in my room I smile. In one of the pictures, You
have the most loving, soft, beautiful look that floods me with smiles of Happi-
ness. In the other You have such a devilish look on Your Happy Face that I can't
keep from laughing. They are both very Happy pictures. I feel completely
distracted by You.

"When I look at these pictures of You here in my room, I smile."

This Happy and naturally Attracted Contemplation is the key that unlocks the Secret of the God-Man. And if you practice feeling-Contemplation of Heart-Master Da, you will notice more and more that He Is your own perfect Happiness, in Person.

When I first came to Heart-Master Da Love-Ananda's Hermitage Ashram[4] at Sri Love-Anandashram in Fiji, I noticed how naturally this occurs.

I stayed in a room next door to the library building. One morning I noticed Heart-Master Da Love-Ananda standing on the library porch. As I watched Him, I silently felt the Great Blessing that is conveyed through the mere sight of Him. His Body Itself Radiates the Silent Fullness of the Mystery. I was filled with Happiness just watching Him.

Then He invited one of the children in the Ashram onto the porch. He stopped what He was doing and bent down to give her every particle of His attention. His eyes were very soft and deep and full of Love, and He touched her with a tenderness I had never seen before. His demonstration of Feeling was so pure and spontaneous and Full that I was easily drawn to feel the Mystery of His Divine Happiness.

Heart-Master Da Love-Ananda has always Given His Great Love and Happiness in special ways to His youngest devotees. He has Blessed quite a number of our children by attending their birth and many others by cradling them with His own Love-Radiant hands just after they were born. He has Mysteriously Healed several of our young children when we were very afraid that they might die. He is always performing the Miracle of Helping children to feel His Love and His Radiant Happiness so that they can be Happy, too. And even though He had always shown us this by His actions, one day He Confessed in words how He Feels about His youngest devotees:

HEART-MASTER DA LOVE-ANANDA: *Children are wonderful. I am in love with children. I am in love with children! I mean deeply in love with them. I love these children. I love their faces. We are profoundly in love with one another. (May 1984)*

I myself saw how true this is of Heart-Master Da one day in 1988. I was helping one of the children at Sri Love-Anandashram by turning the pages of her music while she played the piano for Heart-Master Da.

Because she was looking at the piano keys, she could not see Him looking at her, but I could. I practically stopped breathing. I had never seen any human being look so much in love, so tender, so hopelessly caring as Heart-Master Da did while He watched His young devotee. I felt that I was witnessing the most intimate moment in the universe.

Devotees have often praised Heart-Master Da Love-Ananda for showing us how to love children. He has spent many hours (even hundreds) Instructing us in how to teach our children. He has Written several books for and about young devotees, and He has created a whole Way of life in which they can feel and practice Happiness. He always protects and delights children (and older people) with His Love and His Humor, and He is a true Genius at finding ways to Help everyone feel the Mystery. One day, a devotee thanked Heart-Master Da for all that He has Done for children:

DEVOTEE: Heart-Master Da, I feel profoundly Instructed by Your relationship to children. You constantly enliven them and assume a profound intimacy with them and nurture and love them. It moves me so much to see Your example.

HEART-MASTER DA LOVE-ANANDA: See what I do for them. I preserve them, honor them, nourish them, give them life, give them the Great Vision. This is what I do in every moment of every day of life with everyone who is associated with Me most intimately. . . . The Way of the Heart is a relationship and not techniques. There are practices for which you must be responsible, and there are disciplines, but they are secondary to the essence of this Way, which is relationship, the heart-matter, an intimate matter.

The Way of the Heart is an intimate process. It can only be lived as an intimate heart-matter. If you are going to be called a practicing devotee, then this Way of life must become an intimate matter for you. In that sense you are like children, then. You are preserving the Heart, conserving the Heart, animating it, making it the dominant principle, not allowing the Heart to be destroyed.

DEVOTEE: Heart-Master Da, one other thing that I noticed that is a little thing, but something that impressed me greatly. Even with children You will not compromise anything. When they express some egoic little movement, I have seen You require them to change their action in such a wonderfully compassionate, loving, and humorous way.

HEART-MASTER DA LOVE-ANANDA: Why should I cause them pain by making concessions to their egoity? Why govern them towards stress and isolation? Just so, I will not indulge you in your problem. Straighten up. Take a deep breath. Stand with Me. Become My devotee, and My Mere Presence will instruct you. That is what Spiritual life is about. (December 1986)

Anyone can feel Heart-Master Da Love-Ananda's Mysterious Happiness by listening to His Wise Words and by feeling and Contemplating Him. There is an age-old law that explains why this works: You become what you meditate on. If you Contemplate or meditate on or give your attention to the Divine Happiness and Radiant Love that Shines through and as Heart-Master Da, then you will naturally start to feel unreasonably Happy! If you do this, you will soon find yourself to be Happily in Love with Heart-Master Da—and with everyone. Then you must (and will naturally) help your devotion grow by disciplining your un-Happy tendencies, so that you make room for Happiness only.

THE TWO SIDES
OF LOVE

Heart-Master Da Love-Ananda has told us that there are two ways by which we are helped to grow beyond un-Happiness and become truly strong in feeling the Happiness of the Mystery. He begins by talking about a technique His father used to use in his work as a salesman.

HEART-MASTER DA LOVE-ANANDA:
This is how it works: Two men with entirely different qualities approach the people they are trying to persuade. One plays something like the feminine role of being on the side of the people to whom they are making the sale. He is very sympathetic with them, communicating a sense that he might be able to influence the other guy, who plays the male role, the hard-line, hard-edged approach, pressing them to make a decision.
Although this dynamic is frequently used in salesmanship, the principle is

taken out of life. This same dynamic is what persuades us, moves us on, makes us grow. These two principles are present in every aspect of our lives. One is nurturing and supportive, and it connects us to everything, makes us feel loved, makes us feel familiar, and evokes the loving, radiant disposition in us. The other makes the demand, frustrates us, evokes the capacity in us to overcome an obstacle, deal with ourselves, deal with what is difficult, move into new areas of experience. (April 1984)

Heart-Master Da Love-Ananda has always provided both of the qualities that devotees need in order to grow. He Gives both the Blessing or nurturing quality, which "evokes the loving, radiant disposition in us" (and which He humorously calls His "Beauty Foot"), and the challenging quality, which demands that we grow beyond our comfortable limits (His "Power Foot"). And He has often chided His devotees about being "softies" who do not understand the need for challenge and the need to discipline our tendencies. Instead, we like to think that the practice of Happiness should be as easy as playing softball or going to the store and buying a carton of milk.

All the truly accomplished practitioners and Spiritual heroes throughout history have understood that you cannot really grow without fierce self-discipline. In fact, some practitioners have even begun to feel that self-discipline is so important that they forget that it is only the servant of devotion to Happiness. They become so wrapped up in self-discipline that they lose their sense of humor!

Heart-Master Da has Helped us to understand the value of disciplining un-Happy tendencies and to accept the challenging aspect of life as a very positive virtue. But He always reminds us that discipline (for children or for anyone) only works when it is an act of love:

Children must learn how to live from a spiritual point of view, how to live Ecstatically in the feeling of God. They should be practicing Ecstasy, Happiness. They must understand that Happiness fundamentally is what existence is all about. They must acquire spiritual strength for confronting the limitations of their circumstances, and they should not be permitted to play the threatened neurotic games of not feeling happy and free, and spiritually, emotionally, and physically alive. You must establish them in this positive consciousness. . . .

Establish children in a life-positive consciousness. Occupy them with living, adapting, enjoying, breathing, feeling, and relating to the Mystery or God. We should be helping children to practice Ecstasy. And in the midst of their life of feeling and breathing the Mystery, children need to acquire spiritual strength in relationship to the limits imposed by the body and the world.

There is a fundamental sense of the Living Eternal Principle of Life that will pull children through the very real feeling of being collapsed and threatened. If they have not realized a fundamental position that is positive and transcendental, they will adapt to a weak, threatened relationship to all their functions. . . .

Children must be "up against" themselves. They must be involved in self-transcendence. . . . Children must come to understand that they may be required to do things that they may not want to do. In other words, children must be given the structure in which to learn about both pleasure and pain. If children only lead a life of play, they will never be impressed by truly moral circumstances, nor will they be impressed with the total world of the Divine Reality. They will not see significant things about themselves—except their vital game—and this does not serve them. The being grows through confrontation, difficulty, and demand. . . .

We must be consistent in our service to children all day long. There must be this true or moral demand. Never step aside from it. If we consistently change our expectations of children, they will not change! Introduce requirements and discipline children if they do not meet them. Do this in the midst of a life of loving intimacy, for intimacy is the healing principle. . . .

We must give them the gift of a fundamental emotional disposition of Happiness that is as native to them as feeling and breathing—a spiritual, Happy understanding of the Mystery of life.[5]

WISDOM TRIAL AND THE BRAHMACHARYA VISION QUEST

(or, "Vanquish the Tiger: Roar Like a Lion")

Heart-Master Da has always Worked with more energy than you and I and all our friends put together to Serve His devotees—young and old—with Happiness. But Happiness or Love is also a Feeling that you must learn to practice—it does not just happen to you! That is why Heart-Master Da Love-Ananda, the Teacher of Happiness, asks us all:

> *HEART-MASTER DA LOVE-ANANDA: Now what have you learned in your whole life? Have you learned to feel perfectly? Did you ever go through a period of study in which you learned to feel to Infinity, to feel Absolute Divinity?*

To learn how to play the piano really well or to become a great hockey player or pole vaulter or pizza maker, or even anything at all, you must practice. And not only must you practice, you must accept the guidance of a teacher who has already mastered what you want to learn. Such an expert can inspire you to keep growing and can also correct your mistakes, keeping you pointed in the right direction. If you really want to learn and if you have found a good teacher, then you must also do what your teacher asks. Learning Happiness is no different. It requires dedicated practice and a true teacher.

Since ancient times, and in many different religious traditions, those who want to grow in the never-ending Feeling of the Mystery have found that the fastest and best way to do so is by accepting the guidance and Help of a Heart-Master (or Sat-Guru), Who Is that Feeling, in Person. Such Masters of Happiness serve their devotees in a way that no other kind of teacher can. Since the Master of Happiness is actually Happiness in Person, he or she can transmit the Feeling of Happiness and Mystery to you very directly, even silently, without moving, over long distances, and always. Nevertheless, as you will see Brahmacharini Shawnee learning in these pages, such practice often involves forms of discipline and testing that are difficult, requiring obedience even in circumstances that are not easy to understand at first.

Heart-Master Da Love-Ananda is always Working to give heart-strength to His devotees and to everyone—no matter what they do or how old they are. In fact, He knows that even very young children can receive His Blessing-Transmission and also become strong, even by passing difficult tests if they need to. This is the story of how Heart-Master Da Helped Neem, a young boy of two, learn about being strong and Happy:

Heart-Master Da Love-Ananda has a great voice. It always resounds with Love, whether it is soft as a whisper or booming loud with force. He sings beautifully and He can imitate many different accents so perfectly that you just have to laugh. One day at a gathering with devotees, Heart-Master Da began to speak in a scary "Dracula" voice. Some devotees laughed with delight and some playfully pretended to be scared. But Neem, who could sometimes be withdrawn or afraid, got scared for real. He shrank back.

Heart-Master Da Love-Ananda noticed that Neem was having a hard time. He turned to Neem, still speaking in His Dracula voice, and started coaxing him beyond his fear, telling Neem how great and fun and wonderful it was to make scary noises. Then Heart-Master Da invited Neem to make some scary noises himself. But Neem was too afraid. Heart-Master Da started to roar like a lion, inviting young Neem to roar with Him. Now, Heart-Master Da's roar sounded just as thunderous and awesome as a lion in the jungle, so this was truly a scary noise and quite a test for Neem. But, at the same time, Heart-Master Da was Radiating His Love and Help to Neem—you could see it on His face and feel it in the room. Neem bravely started to roar back. At first Neem's "roars" sounded more like a squeaky kitten. But as he persisted, his roars got bigger and better. Finally, he was strong enough to really roar like a lion with his Heart-Master.

After this, whenever Neem would seem too shy or withdrawn or afraid of life, his parents and friends would ask him to roar like a lion. All of Neem's friends noticed how hard this was for him at first, but they also noticed how Neem was getting stronger and less afraid. He began to feel free to go right up to people and not hold back his energy. He was only two, but Neem had received a Blessing and learned a lesson that would help him for the rest of his life.

Even though it can be trying or scary, it is very important to learn such strength. For example, when zoologist Jane Goodall went to Africa to study chimpanzees in the wild, she noticed one young chimpanzee who was remaining very attached to his mother. Because his mother did everything for him, nothing was requiring this chimpanzee to learn to be strong and to do things for himself. When the mother died, the son did not know what to do. He had not learned to meet the challenge of life on his own. He wandered off into the jungle and died a few weeks later. So you can see that the love that helps a person grow must include challenge, discipline, and demand.

Throughout history, this has been understood in the world's sacred traditions, where the choice to practice Spiritual life is honored and carefully cultivated throughout a child's entire early life. Many religions have made it possible for children who want to devote themselves to God to live in places set aside for the discipline and demand of concentrated practice.

For example, Hildegard of Bingen was an ecstatic practitioner who lived in Germany during the twelfth century. When she was eight years old, she was given by her parents to a convent of Benedictine nuns. She grew up to become a mystic who excelled in the sacred arts, praising God in poetry, music, and painting.

The *Old Testament* tells a story of the child Samuel, who was consecrated, or given over, to God by his mother, Hannah. Hannah brought Samuel to Eli, the high priest, when Samuel was only four, and he grew up to become a religious leader among his people.

Similarly, Marpa the Translator, who was a great Adept and Champion of the Teaching of Wisdom in Tibet, was sent as a youth to live in a monastery because his parents felt that only such a disciplined life could help him channel his uncontrollable energy— especially his anger!

Tibetan Buddhists have even found a way to recognize very young children who show signs of Spiritual advancement carried over from practice in previous lifetimes. They call such children, who are reincarnations of previous religious teachers or Realizers, "tulkus". Rato Khyongla Nawang Losang of Dayab, a district in Tibet, was five years old when four monks came to his house on horseback. They told his parents that they had been led to him by many signs, including the dreams of others and the appearance of a rainbow over his house at the time of his birth. After speaking with his parents, they promised that they would return to take him to their "labrang", or lama's residence, in a year's time. When the monks had left, Rato Khyongla's father told him, "Norbu, my son, you are now a recognized tulku. To all our people and all the monks in Dayab, the name of the Lama Khyongla is a precious gem in the crown of the Buddhist faith, and you are his reincarnation. Soon you must study to improve your mind, so that when you grow up you will be able to act for the benefit of the people of Dayab. May you learn to teach the words of the Lord Buddha as your predecessors did! If you can accomplish this, you will fulfill the most ardent wishes of your parents."[6] On his sixth birthday, Rato began the traditional tulku's life of study and discipline under the guidance of tutors in the monastery. His childhood tutor always reminded him that his special training was not just for him—it was being given to him so that he could in turn serve many others.

Chogyam Trungpa, who was also recognized to be a tulku at a very young age, describes the rigors of the traditional training that such tulkus receive:

I had been brought up very strictly since infancy, from the age of eighteen months, so that I had no other reference point such as the idea of freedom or being loose. I had no idea what it was like to be an ordinary child playing in the dirt or playing with toys or chewing on rusted metal or whatever. Since I did not have any other reference point, I thought that was just the way the world was. I felt somewhat at home, but at the same time I felt extraordinarily hassled and claustrophobic. It did not feel so good.

At the same time I knew that there were little breaks, like going to the bathroom—which was an enormous relief. The only time I was not being watched was when I went to the bathroom. It was my one free time. . . . Apart from that, I was always watched. Even when I ate, I was watched and told how to eat properly, how to extend my arm, how to watch the cup, how to bring it to my mouth. If I made a big noise while swallowing, I was criticized for eating "crocodile style." I was told that rinpoches, or other important tulkus, were not supposed to swallow crocodile style.[7]

Even though it was difficult, he eventually saw that this strict discipline served a very positive purpose:

Then, very interestingly, I stopped struggling with the authorities, so to speak, and began to develop. . . .

Something was actually working. Something was finally beginning to click. The discipline had become part of my system. My tutors and my teachers were pushed by me instead of my being pushed by them. I wanted to know more and more about what was happening, and they began to run out of answers. They were hassled by me because I was so wholehearted. They became afraid that they could not keep up with me anymore. . . .

It is a question of interest. Once you are really into something, you become part of the experience, or it becomes part of you. When you become part of the teachings, you are no longer hassled. You are no longer an entity separate from the teachings. You are an embodiment of them. That is the basic point.[8]

Brahmacharini Shawnee and her friends did not need to take or pass the tests traditionally given to tulkus to determine whether their births were special or whether they have a unique responsibility to practice Happiness for the sake of others, because they have been born into the Gurukula of Sat-Guru Da Love-Ananda. (In Hinduism, the "Gurukula" is the sacred Family of the Guru and it most often includes his closest devotees, his children, and any young devotees he has accepted into his household for the sake of their Spiritual practice.) Because they have lived always in His most intimate Sphere, and especially because Brahmacharini Shawnee and two of her friends are Heart-Master Da Love-Ananda's own daughters, it is already obvious that they have been Given a rare and most precious Gift. And it is also clear, as it is understood in the traditions, that these Brahmacharinis who have been Blessed to be born into the direct Company of the Radiant Heart-Adept and World-Friend, Da Love-Ananda Hridayam, will more and more become an "embodiment" of His Teaching, thus performing a great service to many, many others through the strength of their devotion to Him.

But, no matter how special the circumstances of their birth and despite whatever help they may have received as a child, there comes a moment in the life of each practitioner when all the years of preparation, training, nurture, and care culminate in a crisis. In that moment, we must each stand alone and make our own choice about how we will live and practice. From that point forward, we are each responsible for our own destiny.

Many traditional cultures acknowledge this kind of transition—which is the passage from childhood to adult responsibility. And, in almost every culture, this passage involves a great ordeal of growth and testing. As an example, young people of many American Indian tribes wander the wilderness alone without food, waiting for a vision. They feel, and listen, and look for signs of the spirits of the natural world so that they can contact the spirit that is to be their helper and guide throughout their adult life. By this trial, they learn how to carry the lessons of their childhood forward into greater responsibility in the adult community and deeper feeling-participation in the spirit world.

Brahmacharini Shawnee (and her friends) have been making just this kind of passage. Although the Wisdom-Principle behind their testing is very different from that of an American Indian youth, there are many similarities in the ordeal they have had to undergo.

HEART-MASTER DA LOVE-ANANDA: Only when you pass the trial of manhood, male or female, are you ready for the Wisdom trial. "Kill the tiger", and then go on your vision quest. . . .

Thus, we must introduce a trial, which need not take a traditional form, into the lives of those who grow up in our community. A variety of approaches are worth studying, but our effect on those who become teenagers should be humanizing and should serve their adaptation to true Wisdom, true adulthood, true human responsibility. . . .

If you had killed a tiger or made a hair shirt, if you had had to pass through a trial by fire and grow up, you would make a different society with one another. You would understand the difficulties of life, the possibilities of suffering, the destructive nature of the universe. Then you would exemplify a superior disposition, a truly human capability.

The tiger is the ego, and the tiger is death. You must confront them both.

You must confront yourself and the imposition of the universe, and you must overcome both to be a man, male or female. Then you will be good company, and then you will also continue to grow. (May 1987)

For many years, although Shawnee and her friends did not even realize it, Heart-Master Da Love-Ananda had prepared them to undergo their own unique "vision quest". Then, in the spring of 1988, when Shawnee was thirteen years old, Heart-Master Da Love-Ananda asked her and her friends to make a greater, more adult, and one-pointed commitment to practice Happiness in His Blessing Company. He asked them to enter His "Brahmacharya Order". In extending this invitation, Heart-Master Da was offering them a form of sacred learning that has been highly valued for many, many centuries.

The first brahmacharya schools were to be found in the remote forests of ancient India several thousand years ago. Traditionally, children of the right age and qualification were sent by their parents to live with a brahmacharya master so that they could be taught the value of intimacy with God. The brahmacharis (boys) or brahmacharinis (girls) in those original forest ashram-schools lived a life of religious study, service, and contemplation of God just as all of Heart-Master Da Love-Ananda's

BRAHMACHARYA:
STUDY OF GOD
"Brahma" is a Hindu
term for the One,
All-Including God
or "Immense Being",
and "acharya" means
study.

Brahmacharini Shawnee and her friends have been the first to embrace the ancient, eternal, and yet also always new brahmacharya practice that Heart-Master Da Love-Ananda Offers to all. These original Brahmacharinis of Sri Love-Anandashram belong to a formal Order called The Hridaya Da Gurukula Brahmacharini Mandala. "Hridaya" is a Sanskrit word that means "Heart". Because Heart-Master Da Love-Ananda Is the Perfect and Everlasting Happiness that is at the core, or Heart, of all that exists, He uses this age-old word to refer to His Blessing Work and even to Himself. "Da" means "Giver", and, because He always Gives the Happiness of the Heart to all others, it is another one of His Names. Lastly, because "mandala" means "circle", the name of their Order tells us exactly what these four Brahmacharinis do: They form an intimate circle of self-transcending devotion around Heart-Master Da Love-Ananda Hridayam.

THE HRIDAYA DA GURUKULA BRAHMACHARINI MANDALA, 1989
(top left) Brahmacharini Shawnee, age 13;
(top right) Brahmacharini Io, age 13; (bottom left) Brahmacharini Tamarind, age 13; (bottom right) Brahmacharini Naamleela, age 9

brahmacharya devotees do. All brahmacharis knew that their study was a form of service to the whole community, and that they would be called upon in the future to guide others with the clarity and force of devotion that they developed during the years of their brahmacharya training.

When the time was right, and the prospective brahmachari and his or her parents had been rightly tested and instructed, sacred rites of initiation were performed. From that time forward, the brahmachari honored his or her brahmacharya master as Spiritual teacher and as a guiding parent. Through the gift of his Spiritual benediction and the wisdom of the disciplined life he offered to his students, the brahmacharya master granted each brahmachari a "second birth", or a new life of participation in the sacred Reality.

Heart-Master Da has always Given His young students Great Vision and Great Blessing. And He has always Called them to pass the tests and "meet the mark" of self-transcending Happiness so that they can be "creatively effective, whole, essentially simple, and utterly free of the illusion of separation from what is Real, Divine, Blissful, and Great." And now, in Offering Shawnee and her friends the opportunity to participate in His Brahmacharya Order, He was Offering them a new life—a life of even greater feeling-participation in the Immense Being that is the Mysterious Heart of existence.

TWO SACRED CIRCLES
AND THE SECRET
OF THE KACHINA IN
THE WAY OF THE HEART

Even with this wonderful circumstance, great Help, and venerated Wisdom, however, the brahmacharya practice that Heart-Master Da Love-Ananda has Given these four young girls is not easy! The brahmacharya practice Heart-Master Da Offers to children everywhere is not just a Western version of something that has been done before in the East—the Brahmacharya Way that He has Given to young people today (and forever) is based on a Great Secret that He is the first to Reveal, and that He will Reveal to you in the pages to come. And He has married His

THE HRIDAYA DA GURUKULA KANYADANA KUMARI MANDALA

The name of their Order also describes how the Kanyadana Kumaris have fashioned their lives in response to Heart-Master Da. "Kanya" means purity, "dana" means to give a gift, "kumari" means a virtuous and devout woman. Thus, "The Hridaya Da Gurukula Kanyadana Kumari Mandala" is the circle of women practitioners who have given the gift of lifelong love and devotion to Heart-Master Da Love-Ananda, and whose purity of practice is a gift of inspiration to others.

(top left) Kanya Remembrance, (top right) Kanya Tripura Rahasya, (bottom left) Kanya Kaivalya Navaneeta, (bottom right) Kanya Suprithi

Heart-Secret with the ancient brahmacharya tradition, creating a Way that is happily new and full of time-tested wisdom at the same time.

The four original Brahmacharinis of Sri Love-Anandashram are helped in their practice of Happiness by four other members of Heart-Master Da's Gurukula—the members of the sacred circle called "The Hridaya Da Gurukula Kanyadana Kumari Mandala".

The four Kanyadana Kumaris are very remarkable women who have devoted their lives to serving Heart-Master Da and Realizing His Great Happiness. Through their steadfast devotion, they have discovered Heart-Master Da's Wise Secret, and it has made them very, very Happy. This great Happiness shines through them in many ways—their readiness to praise Heart-Master Da and other people, their easy laughter and capability to find humor even in difficult situations, the way they effortlessly give all their love and attention to whomever they meet (winning the hearts of those they meet by doing so), the way they command respect and will not accept anything less than Happiness from their friends, their calm steadiness in the midst of testing, the very deep way they surrender themselves in meditation and "bathe" in Heart-Master Da Love-Ananda's Gift of Love-Bliss, the way their sacred service always evokes the Feeling of His Heart-Presence, and their one-pointed commitment to serving their Heart-Master. They are very strong and inspiring devotees.

Kanya Remembrance is the principal appointed guide and headmistress of The Hridaya Da Gurukula Brahmacharini Mandala.

Together, the Kanyadana Kumaris and the Brahmacharinis form two circles of devotion and intimate service that surround Heart-Master Da and support His Work to Bless everyone everywhere.

Early in 1988, before Io, Shawnee, Tamarind, and Naamleela took up brahmacharya practice, Heart-Master Da did something that foreshadowed the transforming ordeal that they would soon undergo.

Tamarind has studied ballet for many years. She is a beautiful dancer who dearly loves her art. Each year on her birthday in January, she offers a special dance to Heart-Master Da. On her thirteenth birthday, in 1988, she was faced with a new responsibility: Heart-Master Da had been asking her for several months to find a way to make her dancing a sacred communication about Divine Happiness. When the time for the performance came, she offered Him a dance that was full of the feeling of breaking through limits. It was a self-transcending dance, and it was a good beginning in making her art more sacred.

Heart-Master Da grinned with pleasure and He applauded heartily when she finished her performance, tossing her a flower to Bless her dance. He motioned Tamarind to come to Him, and He Gave her a big hug. Then He quickly reached under His Chair and pulled out a mysterious gift covered with a silken cloth. Everyone gasped as He whisked away the cloth. It was an exquisite, colorful, energetic Kachina doll in a dancing pose! Heart-Master Da told Tamarind that His special Gift of the Kachina doll would help her discover how to make her dancing sacred.

Later, when Tamarind studied about Kachina dolls, she learned that these beautiful carved dolls are traditionally given by Kachinas (the healing priests and spirit-teachers of the Hopi Indians) to the children of the tribe as a way of teaching them about the ancient, secret, and sacred ways of the Hopi people.

By Giving her this Kachina doll, Heart-Master Da (who did not know about this custom) had intuitively done just what the venerable Hopi holy men had always been taught to do. And, because of Heart-Master Da's Guidance, Tamarind was beginning to discover the secret of the ancient Kachinas: To make your art sacred, you have to make your whole life sacred. Tamarind and her friends were about to embark on an adventure

The Kachina doll

and a trial in which they would begin to discover how to do just this.

It was only a few months after Tamarind's dance that Heart-Master Da would initiate her (and her three companions) into the practice of brahmacharya life and these four young practitioners would be required to grow more fully in the sacred Mystery of their relationship to Him. Their "vision quest" had begun: to discover the Great Secret of the Way of the Heart. In this and countless other ways, Heart-Master Da has Helped Brahmacharinis Naamleela, Tamarind, Shawnee, and Io continue to grow in the Mystery—in whatever stage or manner they were ready for.

Heart-Master Da Love-Ananda's Blessing is the greatest Help in living a life that is sane and calm and not afraid and still growing and also filled with Immense Joy. That is why His devotees are full of devotion for Heart-Master Da. Because of our devotion to Him we also practice service, self-discipline, and meditation—for they express the Happiness that Heart-Master Da Gives to all who formally enter into sacred relationship with Him as Sat-Guru.

When the Brahmacharinis saw how much their devotional relationship to Heart-Master Da helped them to Feel Happy, they began to do only what serves their relationship to Him as their Sat-Guru (Full of Heart-Blessing) and their Wise and Inspiring Teacher of Happiness. As a result, they began to practice service, self-discipline, and meditation with greater energy, and their devotion and their response to the Feeling of the Mystery began to grow even stronger.

Through service we can forget un-Happiness by bringing our energy and love to Heart-Master Da and everyone else. Through self-discipline, we can let go of our habits that reinforce un-Happiness. Through meditation, we can feel beyond the crankiness that comes up in our bodies and minds and receive Heart-Master Da Love-Ananda's Great Gift of Heart-Blessing, which allows us to feel and breathe and love and even Be the Feeling of the Mystery. Thus, service, self-discipline, and meditation are ways of Remembering Heart-Master Da Love-Ananda and His Heart-Happiness.

Brahmacharya discipline (and even adult practice) in the Way of the Heart revolves around an enlivening, heart-awakening, and challenging daily schedule of devotional practice (including meditation, ceremonies of sacred worship, readings from Heart-Master Da's Teaching, chanting, and meditation), as well as study of His Wisdom-Teaching and discriminative study of the teachings of all the world's great religions, Yoga and calisthenics in the form of "conscious exercise",[9] academic learning, sports, and sacred arts.

Heart-Master Da has told us of the Wisdom and the purpose underlying these practices:

We must give our children the cause and freedom to be Ecstatic. Children must understand what Ecstasy is, what Happiness is. Parents and teachers should discover the functional dimension to which children are sensitive at every stage of adaptation, and then teach them in those functional terms. . . .

We must help children become sensitive to other people and teach them how to cooperate and serve in all their relations. Also, children should learn to bring feeling and sensitivity to the meditative exercise, as given in What and Where and Who To Remember To Be Happy [10] *and to other devotional practices appropriate to their stage of life.*[11] *These activities serve the process of the child's relationship to the Mystery of existence. . . .*

Children should be talking about Spiritual life, about the Mystery. . . .

They should be talking and learning about Spiritual Teachers, and studying moral, religious, and Spiritual stories. Children should be introduced, constantly and all day long, to a non-ordinary way of life. Find a way to make their lessons aligned to the Teaching of Truth and with this Spiritual Way of life. Their lessons should have moral and Spiritual significance, and children should be instructed not in a way that merely impresses them, but that truly awakens their understanding. . . . Children are involved in a spiritual struggle, working out a spiritual problem. Therefore, all children should be Ecstatic and awake, consorting bodily with the Feeling of the Mystery.[12]

Profound understanding of the realities of life, the capability to feel Divine Happiness and be surrounded by people who help you to feel This all the time, all the opportunities and tests that you need to grow—these are all great Gifts that Heart-Master Da Offers to everyone who responds to Him. But even before all these is His first Gift—the Happiness and Mystery and Love-Radiant Feeling that wakes up in your heart and your eyes and your life when you see and feel the God-Man Da Love-Ananda Hridayam Shining His Blessing to you and all. For the Divine Master Da always wanders Freely in the Infinite Mystery, extending His Radiant Being to us as a Bridge by which we may pass to Perfect Happiness.

We hope that, by reading these stories, you will be moved to Feel the Measureless Bliss hidden in the Heart-Secret of Da, the One Who Gives. Then you may know the necessity of, and even someday embrace, the wise and demanding discipline of Happiness that forever unlocks His Secret in your own heart.

Heart-Master Da Love-Ananda, 1990

ABOUT
THE WORLD-TEACHER, HEART-MASTER DA LOVE-ANANDA

"Smelling the Moon"

The Story of His Life of Spiritual Heroism and Divine Blessing

Heart-Master Da's early life was filled with many unusual and delightful incidents that pointed to the fact that He is not like ordinary people. When He was a young boy, He spent many hours in the woods around the town where He grew up and in His backyard. Although He had many friends, He also loved the solitude and the wild feeling of nature. One day while He was adventuring outside, He started to imagine things that He liked. He began to notice that if He concentrated on whatever He was imagining, He could smell it as if it were right in front of His nose. He did this over and over again—enjoying the smells of his favorite things.

When He asked His friends if they could do this too, they told Him that it had never occurred to them to try. So they immediately set about imagining things and trying to smell them. Even though they enjoyed the experiment, no one could do it. Although this was just one small incident in a childhood filled with remarkable Events and Divine Awareness, Heart-Master Da has said that this game helped Him to realize that He was not the same as His friends.

For Heart-Master Da Love-Ananda is a "God-Born" Adept, a Divinely Realized Being who Freely and Compassionately Chose to assume human Form to help others discover Happiness. Thus, the Story of Heart-Master Da's Life and Work is full of Mystery and Revelation and Great Bravery.

His unique Divine Nature showed Itself in many magical ways. At times, in the forest with His friends or when He was alone, His body would float in the air and, sometimes, He would even fly! He could see the future and, at times, He would surprise His friends by telling them exactly what they were thinking! But, despite the fact that these unusual powers could be very delightful, they were not Heart-Master Da Love-Ananda's most important pastime.

While He was still very young, Heart-Master Da became aware that the purpose of His Life was to Serve the Happiness of others. One day, while He was walking to the movies with His mother and father, the two of them began to argue. He remembers:

. . . there was a bright full moon, orange and shadowy, and I am not sure what movie we were on our way to see. I must have been about five or six years old.

What appeared to me then was a kind of archetype of all conflict. There was separation, which was destroying the energy of enjoyment or love. And I was about to make one of my earliest attempts to communicate that there was only this love. I very clearly and directly experienced the effects of this conflict and separation. I could feel the embracive rays of energy that surrounded us and moved in a delicate network of points in and through our bodies being cut, and dark vacuums were being spotted out around us and between us.

I remember silently expanding this love and trying to distract them by pointing out the moon and asking questions about God and life so they would be calmed and feel the energy of the "bright" in them.

Their humor did return a little. My father seemed quiet-ed, and my mother was answering my questions. We went to the movie, and all the while I felt a pressure in my solar plexus and my heart, where the love-energy was pushed back. But I think the argument was gone after that. . . .

It was at least that early in my life that I perceived (in the "bright") the guiding purpose in my life: to restore humor.[1]

All His life, Heart-Master Da has Worked to Touch others with this love and humor. One night, He spoke to His devotees in words of poetry and ecstasy about His Impulse to Give everyone the Gift of His Heart-Happiness. He told us, "Now and forever, I Transmit My Blessing through loveliness, intimacy, close talk beyond words, smelling the moon, you know?" And He Called us to let everyone know about the Love-Great Mystery of His Blessing, "Pass the torch on to the one next to you and to your children, your friends, all the world." He had told us and also proved to us by His every action that, more than anything, He Loves to see others being Happy. Now, on this night of paradoxical speeches, He coaxed and invited us to be Happy with Him, to "smell the moon", and to show Him that we would pass His Blessing—the Blessing He had been Born to Give to everyone—on to many others. "Let Me see the center of the moon," He said, reminding us (in Mysterious terms) of His Desire to see everyone Happy, "Let Me see thousands making the God-Sign and transforming the life of humankind. Let Me Love it."

Another way of understanding the Great Work of Blessing that Heart-Master Da Love-Ananda does for you and everyone is to learn about His Names. Heart-Master Da Love-Ananda's formal Name, "The Naitauba Avadhoota, Hridaya-Samartha Sat-Guru Da Love-Ananda Hridayam", and His Title, "The World-Teacher", tell the story of Who He Is and What He Gives.

"Avadhoota" is a word from Sanskrit, an ancient and very sacred language of India. It means a person who is Free. It applies to Heart-Master Da because He has "shaken off" every trace of un-Happiness. Because this is so, He does not live like ordinary men and women, always search-ing for Happiness. Heart-Master Da Lives primarily on "Naitauba" (Nye-TUHM-buh), which is the Fijian name of the island that has become His principal Hermitage Ashram. (Now Naitauba is also called "Sri Love-Anandashram".)

"Hridayam" is also a Sanskrit word, which means "The Center is

Here". It describes the Divine Heart or Center of Being that lives every creature and every thing. If you look at Heart-Master Da and open the "feeling eyes" of your heart to see and feel Who He Is in Truth, you will be made extremely Happy. You will notice that He is always Standing in your own heart, Radiating as the same Freedom and Happiness that you are too.

A "Sat-Guru" is one who leads others from the darkness of un-Happiness to the Light of perfect Truth, or the Heart Itself. A "Samartha" Sat-Guru has immense Powers of Blessing and Help to use in Awakening devotees to this Truth. Heart-Master Da is called "Hridaya-Samartha" Sat-Guru because He does His Work of Heart-Awakening by the Great Power of the Heart Itself. And He Awakens devotees to feel and even Be Who He Is, which is "Love-Ananda" ("Divine Love-Bliss"). As Divine World-Teacher (or, in Sanskrit, "Jagad-Guru"), Heart-Master Da Gives His perfect Wisdom and Heart-Blessing to everyone, everywhere.

So, if we were to distill the meaning of all His Names and Titles into a very short description of Who Heart-Master Da Is and What He Does for devotees, it would be this: He is the Free Realizer Who Uses the Blessing Power of the Heart to Give everyone in the world the Gift of Love-Bliss, or Happiness Itself. In this book, you will hear some of the countless stories His devotees have to tell about exactly how He does this Miraculous Work.

BORN AS THE "BRIGHT"

In His autobiography, *The Knee of Listening*, Heart-Master Da describes the remarkable State He lived in as an infant (and that He has always Communicated to others):

Even as a baby I remember only crawling around inquisitively with an incredible sense of joy, light, and freedom in the middle of my head that was bathed in energies moving freely down from above, up, around, and down through my body and my heart. It was an expanding sphere of joy from the heart. And I was a radiant form, a source of energy, bliss, and light in the midst of what is entirely energy, bliss, and light. I was the power of Reality, a direct enjoyment and communication. I was the Heart, who lightens the mind and all things. I was the same as every one and every thing, except it became clear that others were apparently unaware of the thing itself.[2]

Heart-Master Da as a baby

For the first two years of His Life, Heart-Master Da lived as this "Bright" Divine Being. He associated with His physical body, but He did not come fully all the way "down" into it. He saw that the world and everything and everyone in it were One with the "Bright" of Consciousness or Happiness Itself. But He began to see that the "Bright" and Its Joy are not noticed or allowed in the world. So, when He was two years old, He made a Mysterious and Heroic sacrifice. He descended into the body and identified with the personality of "Franklin Jones" (the name given to Him by his parents).

HEART-MASTER DA LOVE-ANANDA: Franklin Jones, as a limited condition, began one day while I was crawling across the linoleum floor in a house that my parents had rented from an old woman named Mrs. Farr. There was a little puppy dog that my parents had gotten for me running across the floor towards me. I saw the puppy dog, and I saw my parents, and it began from that moment. All the rest of the events which occurred during the two or more years prior to that were not the years of Franklin Jones. He has no existence prior to that time, the conscious or intentional beginning. (April 1974)

"I saw the puppy dog, and I saw my parents, and it began from that moment."

As "Franklin", Heart-Master Da began His unique Sacred Ordeal of Service to others. He was deeply moved by the un-Happiness He saw all around Him, and He had even let go of the "Bright" so that He could Feel what it was like to live without it. By this brave Gesture, He set about discovering what would be required for ordinary people to be restored to the Freedom and Joy of the "Bright".

**Boyhood family home
on Long Island**

Heart-Master Da Love-Ananda (now "Franklin") grew up in Franklin Square, a small town on Long Island about twenty-five miles east of New York City. He lived with His father, Frank (who was a salesman), His mother, Dorothy (a housewife), and a sister, Joanne, eight years younger. A number of uncles, aunts, and cousins lived nearby and shared many family occasions with them.

As a growing boy, Heart-Master Da found many other ways to bring His Enjoyment and Humor to His friends and relatives. He liked to lead His neighborhood friends in adventures in the woods that surrounded Franklin Square. He recited poems, sang, and told stories. He made a puppet theater in His parents' cellar and put on shows for the neighbors and their children and His relatives. He became a ventriloquist and performed comedy with His dummy at school and at the local hospital. He loved to draw and paint, and to bring pleasure to others through what He made. Although the "Bright" was no longer His constant experience, the Reality of the "Bright" remained the underlying substance of His Life, like the ground that nurtures a growing tree. The "Bright"

**Heart-Master Da
with His parents and sister**

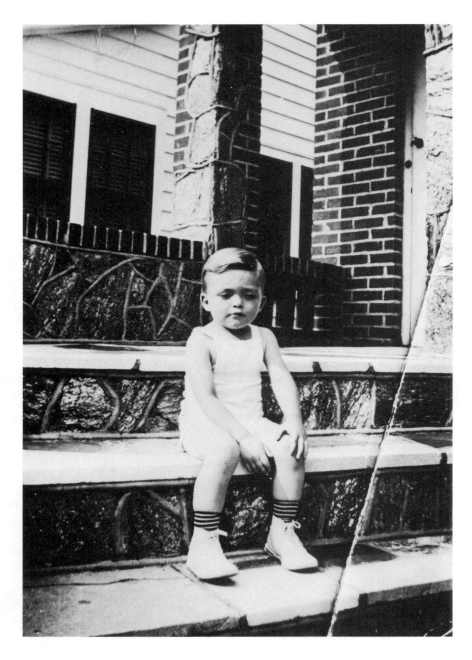

Heart-Master Da as a young boy

was Working to make "Franklin's" body and mind strong and ready for the Liberating Work He had come to do.

Sometimes that Great Power could not be contained by His body, and Heart-Master Da would experience sudden fevers or illnesses that the doctors who examined Him could not explain. From time to time, the "Bright" would break through into His Awareness and He would unexpectedly fall into moods of Ecstasy. Sometimes in Sunday school when the Pastor of the Lutheran Church He attended would read parables about Jesus, Heart-Master Da Love-Ananda would quietly swoon in the Great and Happy Feeling of the Mystery.

When He was a teenager, the Feeling of the "Bright" would suddenly become so strong that He would lose all sense of who or where He was.

HEART-MASTER DA LOVE-ANANDA: Look one another in the eye, face to face, and you will be like my high school girlfriend and me, standing on the doorstep many years ago. In my teenage years at times I would be with someone with whom I was totally familiar, not only this girlfriend, but others also, and suddenly I would have no sense whatsoever of where I was, who I was, or who he or she was. In other words, I would have no sense of familiarity, no sense of recognition. In my teenage years these were the breakthroughs of the Prior Being, or Transcendental Enlightenment. (October 1982)

Lutheran church in Franklin Square

Heart-Master Da in His teenage years

On those occasions, He only floated in the Blissful Mystery that Lives all things, and in which no separate beings even exist!

FRANKLIN FOLLOWS THE "BRIGHT"

When He was 18, Heart-Master Da left His family home to go to Columbia College, in New York City. He attended classes, as all college students do, but He had a different purpose than His fellow students. He wanted to recapture the "Bright" and to discover what He had to do to live always in that Freedom once again. Throughout His years in college and the following years of graduate school at Stanford University in California, the Consciousness or Happiness of the "Bright" continued to re-assert Itself, in more and more dramatic moments of crisis and break-through.

On one extraordinary night when He was in His junior year at Columbia, after He had tried everything He could think of to recapture the Power and Happiness of the "Bright", Heart-Master Da had an experience that changed the course of His life. In a flash of great joy and understanding, He saw that His search for the "Bright" would never work, because Truth and Happiness cannot be found by someone who thinks or feels that they have been lost. He saw that the very idea or presumption that the "Bright" was missing and that He needed to find it was not true—because, as He says, ". . . we are, at any moment, always and already free." This discovery that Truth or Happiness are always already the case made Heart-Master Da Love-Ananda Brilliantly Happy.

After this experience, Heart-Master Da began to feel that we are all controlled by a hidden drama or script that is not even true. By now, Heart-Master Da Love-Ananda was in His early twenties, living in a small house on the beach in northern California. He decided to concentrate all His energies in discovering exactly what this Happiness-preventing script

During His years in college

is. He became a kind of Spiritual detective, looking everywhere for clues that would reveal the fake drama that keeps us bound to un-Happiness. He noticed, and then wrote down, everything that happened around Him, both in the environment He lived in and even in His own mind. Heart-Master Da describes this practice of witnessing and writing:

Every creature or environment I perceived became a matter of profound attention. I would write long pages of exhaustive observation on every step of a walk on the beach, or the day-long process and change of the ocean. There was page after page describing the objects and marks in the sand as I walked, detailed descriptions of rooms, mental environments, etc.[3]

Finally, His investigation began to reveal the story at the root of all our wandering from Happiness. Heart-Master Da saw that we live just like Narcissus in the Greek myth.

This is how this story (of unnecessary tragedy and loss) has been told since ancient times: Narcissus was the fair beloved of all the gods, but he chose to wander on his own, seeking something greater. He came upon a still pool of water in the woods and, gazing down, saw his own reflection in the pond. Thinking that this image was someone else, he fell in love with it and spent the rest of his days there at the water's edge like a perfect fool, spellbound by his own image. Narcissus was unable to look up and respond to the actual, living relationship offered to him by others all around. He died alone.

Ever since Heart-Master Da discovered the significance of the myth of Narcissus, He has used this story to describe how we put all our attention on the mirage of our own separate sense of "I" and "me" and "mine", rather than living as self-forgetting love in all relationships. Because we are so wrapped up in this false idea or myth, we have no attention left over to delight in what is Real—which is the "Bright" Itself.

Heart-Master Da Love-Ananda is a very keen observer of life. His sensitivity to the Real Nature of things enabled Him to find guidance from many unusual sources in His pursuit of the Truth. This is how He came to learn from Robert the cat, who was to become a very special friend and even a teacher of natural wisdom. During the years when Heart-Master Da was observing the patterns of His own life and mind to uncover the myth of Narcissus, He also watched as Robert roamed the wilderness on the beach.

Robert

I watched him with fascination. I followed him through woods and watched him hunt. I tried to understand his curious avoidance of the sea, and how he could sit on the cliff above the sea, watching the evening sun, and the wind blowing his hairs heroically about his head. The mystery of his pattern of living, his ease and justice, the economy of all his means, the untouchable absence of all anxiety, the sudden and adequate power he brought to every circumstance without exceeding the intensity required, all of his ways seemed to me an epitome of the genius of life. . . . And I loved him as deeply as the universe itself.[4]

Robert was one of many influences, natural and human, that gradually showed the Wisdom of the "Bright" to Heart-Master Da. And when Heart-Master Da understood the script of "Narcissus", He was ready to find His first human Teacher.

THE GREAT LINE OF TEACHERS AND LESSONS IN HEART-MASTER DA LOVE-ANANDA'S SACRED ORDEAL

Heart-Master Da began to have visions that showed Him where He would find His Teacher. Following His vision, Heart-Master Da found Swami Rudrananda (also known as Rudi), in person, in a small Oriental art store in New York City. At the end of their first meeting, Rudi shook

His hand, and Heart-Master Da could feel His body fill up with Spiritual energy. He knew He had found His Teacher.

For the next several years, Heart-Master Da was an exemplary student, doing everything that Rudi asked of Him, no matter how difficult it was or how much He would have preferred to do something else. He loved and trusted Rudi to guide and help Him. Because of this, Heart-Master Da gave Himself up to Rudi "as a man does to God."

Rudi Taught Heart-Master Da an intense discipline of surrender, or opening up to what Rudi called the "Force". This discipline helped Heart-Master Da to prepare for the higher stages of Spiritual life. Rudi's instructions to Heart-Master Da, which could be summarized in the word "work", required Heart-Master Da to engage His job and relationships and even meditation as a Spiritual practice of intentionally giving up His "self". Under Rudi's guidance, Heart-Master Da grew stronger and healthier and more balanced.

Rudi sat in formal meditation occasions with his students, and during these he transmitted Spiritual energy, or the "Force", to them. Over time, Heart-Master Da grew to feel Rudi's Transmission of the "Force" more and more strongly. In this way, Rudi confirmed for Heart-Master Da that the experiences of the "Bright" He had always had were real and very valuable.

Before long, Heart-Master Da had fulfilled all the disciplines that Rudi had given Him and learned all that Rudi had to offer. He began to feel that the form of effortful surrender that Rudi Taught was no longer necessary for Him.

Swami Rudrananda
("Rudi")

Then one summer day while studying at the Christian seminary that Rudi had asked Him to attend, Heart-Master Da suddenly began to feel as though He were about to die. Although He desperately tried, He could not prevent the fear and the feeling of approaching death. During His classes that day and over the next three days, the fear grew and grew to a point of overwhelming crisis, until finally He let go and allowed the death to happen—and He even watched it happen! He saw that even though the body, the mind, and the personality He usually thought of as himself had died, He remained. Now He knew that the fundamental Reality of the

"Bright" could never die—it was only "Narcissus" who had come to an end.

He walked around and "beamed joyfully at the room". "Narcissus" was dead. Now He understood that there was really nothing to fear and that no one could ever really be separate from the "Bright". He saw that "there is only relationship, only love" and that no effort is required for love. In fact, He saw that no matter what may appear to be happening, there is only the "Bright".

Shortly after this event, Heart-Master Da Love-Ananda came upon some writings by Rudi's Guru, Swami Muktananda. Heart-Master Da was attracted to the Teachings of Swami Muktananda because they stressed the importance of easefully accepting the Grace of the Guru. This was different from Rudi's Teaching about surrender through effort and work. With Rudi's permission, Heart-Master Da traveled to Swami Muktananda's Ashram in Ganeshpuri, a small town in India, to receive Swami Muktananda's Initiation.

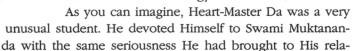

Swami Muktananda was a master of a highly prized form of Yoga, and he initiated in Heart-Master Da many visions and blissful experiences of the extraordinary Energy of the "Bright". (Swami Muktananda called this Energy "the Shakti".)

As you can imagine, Heart-Master Da was a very unusual student. He devoted Himself to Swami Muktananda with the same seriousness He had brought to His relationship with Rudi. He was very responsive to Swami Muktananda's Grace, and everyone at the Ashram was amazed that a Westerner could so quickly have such deep experiences of the Shakti.

Swami Muktananda

When Heart-Master Da began to practice under Swami Muktananda's guidance, the Swami encouraged Heart-Master Da to also accept the Spiritual Blessings of another great Indian Saint, Swami Nityananda, who had served as Guru to both Swami Muktananda and Rudi. (Even though Swami Nityananda's body had already died, his Spiritual influence was still alive.) On His first visit to Swami Muktananda's Ashram,

Swami Nityananda

Heart-Master Da Love-Ananda also had contact with another Spiritual Teacher, Rang Avadhoot. When Heart-Master Da saw Rang Avadhoot in the Ashram garden, Rang Avadhoot communicated strong Spiritual energy to Him through the eyes. At the end of Heart-Master Da's first visit, because of the Blessings of Rang Avadhoot, Swami Muktananda, and Swami Nityananda (and because of His own Feeling of the "Bright"), Heart-Master Da fell into a Swoon of Happiness (called "Samadhi" in Sanskrit) that took Him up to the "Bright" Space of Happiness that is far beyond the body and the mind. When He came back to "normal" awareness after this Blissful experience, Heart-Master Da was very grateful that His Intuition of Divine Happiness had been so directly confirmed.

Rang Avadhoot

A year later, on Heart-Master Da's second visit to the Ashram, Swami Muktananda wrote a letter acknowledging Heart-Master Da's Spiritual Accomplishment and Granting Him permission to Teach others. But Heart-Master Da was looking for more than the energies and visions of the Shakti. He wanted to feel the "Bright", Free and Pure, and He wanted to feel It all the time.

Heart-Master Da with Swami Muktananda

On His third visit to Swami Muktananda's Ashram, Heart-Master Da often walked down the road to the neighboring Ashram where Swami Nityananda had lived. Swami Nityananda was the acknowledged "Parama Guru", or the highest Guru and the source of Spiritual Blessing, in Heart-Master Da's line of Teachers, including Swami Muktananda and Rudi. When Heart-Master Da meditated at the shrine where Swami Nityananda was buried, this is what He felt:

The Shakti was powerfully and freely Present there, and I felt that this place was the source for my instruction now. When I would sit there the Force would surge through my body, my heart and mind would become still, my head and eyes would become swollen with a tremendous magnetic energy, and I would simply relax and enjoy the silent depth of consciousness in that Presence.[5]

Shortly after Heart-Master Da began to receive the blessings of Swami Nityananda most directly, the Shakti miraculously appeared to Him, not in meditation or in the form of energies as before, but in subtle vision, as a Living Person—the "Great Woman", or Goddess, that many people in India worship as the Living Form of Divine Energy! Heart-Master Da felt a strong and devoted love for Her, and He returned to Swami Nityananda's shrine to ask permission to accept Her Guidance. Swami Nityananda gave Heart-Master Da instructions, communicating with Him at the level of subtle feeling.

Swami Nityananda instructed Me to renounce all the Gurus in the Line, including Himself, by performing a sacred ceremony at the shrine of the Goddess, which He Himself had established near Ganeshpuri. He directed Me that by this act of relinquishment I was to surrender My relationships as they were to Swami Nityananda, Swami Muktananda, and Rudi, and accept the Goddess as My Guru. By directing Me to make this act of relinquishment, Swami Nityananda affirmed to Me that the Goddess Herself, Who is only Revealed in rare, unique cases, was in fact His Guru and the Guru of the Lineage. It was therefore the natural progress to be passed from Swami Nityananda to the Goddess, just as I had been passed, in the traditional manner, to Swami Muktananda from Rudi. On that day in the small temple of the Goddess I made the offering of Nityananda and all the Gurus in the Line and fully surrendered into the Guru-Devotee relationship with the Goddess, in Person, Whom I refer to as "Ma". (January 1989)

The Goddess Ma led Heart-Master Da Love-Ananda on a pilgrimage to many of the holy places of the Middle East and Europe, and finally, to Los Angeles.

The image of the Divine Goddess that Heart-Master Da found near Swami Muktananda's Ashram

He was now thirty years old. In Hollywood, Heart-Master Da found a small temple of the Vedanta Society, dedicated to the late Indian Saint Ramakrishna. He was surprised to find that the Vedanta Temple was a potent source of Divine Grace. It was a Spiritual oasis in the midst of the city, and He went there often.

One day as He meditated there, He spontaneously fell into a deep state of Blissful and Infinite Being. He felt Himself become Consciousness, or Happiness Itself. He took on the form of Siva, who is known in the Hindu tradition as the Divine Being Who stands Motionless, Free, and Unchanging, before all forms and events. Then He felt the Presence of the Mother Shakti as the Divine Energy that moves all forms and events in the universe. They Embraced one another and Merged as One. As they combined with One another, the Energy of the Divine Shakti and the Consciousness of the Divine Self became the One Self-Radiant Divine Person. The Shakti that Heart-Master Da had contacted in meditation when He studied with Rudi and Swami Muktananda and to Whom He had been given by Swami Nityananda was no longer Guru and Guide to Him. Instead, She had become His Loved One, and He held Her forever to His heart.

The Vedanta Temple, Hollywood, California

The next day, Heart-Master Da returned to the temple and waited for the Shakti to show Herself again. But nothing happened. There was nothing else that could possibly happen. He was already perfectly established as the "Bright", the Perfect Happiness of Love-Bliss Itself. Now He saw that what He had always sought had been Accomplished.

I simply sat in the temple and knew what I am. I was being what I am. I am Truth, the Divine Self, the One who lives and breathes all things and all beings. I am the Radiant Divine Being, known as God, Happiness, Love, the Mystery.[6]

As Heart-Master Da had grown with the help of His Teachers, He had been passed in the traditional manner along the Line from Rudi to Rudi's Teacher, Swami Muktananda, and from Swami Muktananda to Swami Muktananda's Teacher, Swami Nityananda, who in turn gave Heart-Master Da to the Shakti, Revealing Her to be the True Spiritual Source in the Line of all Heart-Master Da Love-Ananda's Teachers. In the marvel of Her surrender to Him in the Vedanta Temple, the Great Goddess Ma Revealed that Heart-Master Da Himself was now the Parama Guru in the line of His Teachers and the True Sat-Guru and Ever-Blessing Source of Grace. From that moment forward, Heart-Master Da's miraculous Powers to Bless and Awaken others spontaneously began to show themselves.

After His Re-Awakening in the Vedanta Temple, 1970

THE "BRIGHT" WARRIOR
IN A WORLD OF DRAGONS
AND HIS GRAND VICTORY

When Heart-Master Da came home from the Vedanta Temple on that miraculous day, He said nothing to anyone about what had happened. But from that moment on, He began to notice many remarkable changes in His own Being. When He sat down to meditate, as He had for many years, He no longer saw the content of His own mind and psyche. Instead, He saw that He was now meditating countless beings. Over time, some of the people He saw in meditation began to appear in His life and ask Him for Spiritual Guidance. And so it was that He spontaneously began to Teach.

But just as every kind of learning requires work, so also every kind of teaching requires work. And Teaching others to let go of un-Happiness is the most difficult Teaching Work of all. Heart-Master Da began to notice that His devotees did not understand how to relate to Him as their Sat-Guru. While He was re-discovering the "Bright" for our sake, Heart-Master Da had always lived as the perfect Devotee. He embraced each of His Teachers in the traditional manner—with great respect and love and unfailing obedience. Heart-Master Da's devotees did not show the signs of exemplary practice and devotion, as He had with His Teachers. Because of this, they did not grow quickly in their practice. They needed even more Help! In His unfailing and Courageous commitment to bring Happiness to others, Heart-Master Da became willing to Teach (for a time) in a unique way—combining Himself with those of us who sought His Help. He took the name "Bubba Free John" ("Bubba" means brother), and He consented to live among us as a serving brother. He appeared to be like us, reserving no part of Himself from the struggle to vanquish our un-Happiness. He did the Work of a passionate Hero, performing miracles of transformation and heedlessly enduring great wounds of neglect and even abuse in the battle to free us from the grip of "Narcissus".

In fact, the story of Narcissus can help us to understand why His Teaching Work was so difficult. In that ancient parable of un-Happiness, the lovely lady Echo calls to Narcissus across the water, inviting him to join her and share her love. But even Echo, with her arms open to him, could not distract Narcissus from his fascination with his own image. And so it was with us. Heart-Master Da's great challenge was to get us to look up from the pond of "I" and "me" and "mine". This is how He describes it:

HEART-MASTER DA LOVE-ANANDA: My Life is a little bit like going into the world of enemies and dragons to liberate somebody who has been captured. You cannot just sit down and tell a dragon the Truth. You must confront a dragon. You must engage in heroic effort to release the captive from the dragon. This is how I Worked in the theatre of My relating to people, particularly in the earlier years, and in the unusual

Heart-Master Da spent many years in His loving, brotherly Struggle to free us from the myth of Narcissus.

involvements of My Life and Teaching. You could characterize it as the heroic Way of Teaching, the way of identifying with devotees and entering into "consideration" in that context and bringing them out of enemy territory, gradually waking them up. (August 1982)

Heart-Master Da spent many years in His loving, brotherly struggle to free us from the myth of Narcissus. He worked constantly to help us see that we could just stop choosing and doing un-Happiness and be Happy instead, as He had done. But we were reluctant to give up our habits of un-Happiness.

Then, in 1979, Heart-Master Da came to

In 1979 as "Da", " the Giver"

fully understand the unique and Divine Powers of Love and Blessing that were at Work in and as and through Him, and His Teaching Work began to change. Heart-Master Da began to Call devotees to a more sacred response to Him. He began to Instruct us in ceremonial worship, in devotional singing, and in the art of prayer—all as expressions of our relationship to Him as the Blessing Source of Happiness Itself. And, as a Sign of the forever Giving Heart-Strength of His Own Person, He Revealed His true Name, "Da", "the Giver". When we received the Gift of this new Name, we knew that it was Perfect. (He once told us that Robert the cat had been the first to call Him by this, His real Name.)

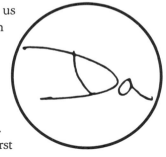

Heart-Master Da's Compassion continued to fuel the years of Teaching He was still to do. Then on January 11, 1986, sixteen years after it began, His Teaching Work suddenly completed itself. When He had done everything and said everything that He possibly could as Teacher (even many times), His frustration that devotees would not fully accept His Gift of self-forgetting Happiness became overwhelming. In His frustration, the "Bright" Itself invaded the Body of Heart-Master Da Love-Ananda so profoundly that He seemed to die. But that Event, which looked like death to those around Him, was not a loss or an ending—rather, it was the beginning of a process that has great significance for the entire world. For when the living energies returned, Heart-Master Da's Body and His entire Being had become the Living Form of the "Bright". His great struggle to get others to understand and give up their un-Happiness was no longer necessary. Now the mere feeling-sight of His Radiant Form had the Power to banish "Narcissus" and restore the heart to Happiness.

A tremendous Infilling or "Swoon" of Love-Bliss had dissolved the Teacher in Him. Now, when we saw His bodily (human) Form with the feeling eyes of the heart, we had to notice that Contemplation of Heart-Master Da's Form was enough to draw us to feel the Mystery.

Heart-Master Da Love-Ananda describes the change that took place in Him:

Suddenly, in the midst of this swoon, there was no more of despair or giving the body up to death. I was, as always, simply Standing In and As My own Nature. This desperate swoon, as if to die, became a spontaneous turnabout in My Disposition, and a unique Spiritual Event was initiated in the midst of that swoon. And that Spiritual Event is still continuing.

Heart-Master Da after His Divine Emergence, 1986

What actually occurred on the morning of January 11, 1986, was a sudden and spontaneous Transition from My Teaching Work to My Blessing Work (or, to My Work As the eternally Free-Standing and always presently Emerging World-Teacher, or "Jagad-Guru"). . . . It is a matter of simply Standing As I Am, while this apparent body-mind is thereby Surrendered utterly into My own Self-Condition. And, by My thus Standing Free, My Work has ceased to be a Struggle to Submit My Self to mankind, one by one, and It has become instead a universally effective Blessing Work, in which mankind, in the form of each and all who respond to Me, must, one by one, surrender, forget, and transcend self in Me.[7]

Over all the years of His Teaching Work, Heart-Master Da lived on the basis of His Impulse to wake others up to Happiness. At times, when He spoke about His great Commitment to the Happiness of others, He told us:

I wish I could kiss every human being on the lips, embrace each one, and enliven each one from the heart.

This Impulse to "kiss" and enliven everyone (which is really a way of describing His Love and His Divine Wish of Happiness for all) has always created Heart-Master Da's Life and Work. But one person cannot possibly embrace every other person on Earth. No matter how hard He tried, Heart-Master Da knew that it was impossible to do this personally, bodily with each one. But now, in what He has called His "Divine Emergence" (which is His name for the Process in which His Teaching Work died and His Blessing Work as Divine World-Teacher Emerged), He discovered a way to fulfill His Great Impulse. In the Mysterious Event of January 11, 1986, the method by which His Heart-Kiss could be Given to all was Revealed. For Heart-Master Da, this was a Grand Victory.

I used the metaphor of kissing to describe My Impulse to serve everyone, all the billions, directly. It was an obvious impossibility as a physical matter. But in that Event it was accomplished. It became simply possible for everyone to respond to Me. Rather than having to move about assuming the likeness of every individual for their sake, I have, by totally bringing this Realization fully into the context of this Body, established a Vehicle that serves everyone if they will give their attention to Me. This is the method of the kiss. (December 1988)

Heart-Master Da Love-Ananda, 1990

❖ *THE TWO SECRETS (yours, AND <u>MINE</u>)*

What a Great Mystery! Through His Great Love and His Willingness to do all that can possibly be done in Service to others, Heart-Master Da brought the Heart-Power of Divine Happiness most Fully Alive in His Own Form. And that is why devotees cherish and celebrate the great practice of feeling-Contemplation of the "Bright" Adept Da Love-Ananda Hridayam. For it is exactly as the Heart-Revealing Adept Da has said:

All My Secrets Are Only Me!
There Is Only One Necessary Revelation, Only One Great Sign To Be Acknowledged and Embraced, Only One Perfect Truth To Be Realized.
I Am The Secret.
I Am The Revelation.
I Am The One To Be Heard and Seen.
Realization Is Realization Of Me.[8]

THE STORY

· · ·

AND
THE
SECRETS

Heart-Master Da Love-Ananda with members of the Hridaya Da Gurukula

Setting the Stage

Four Brahmacharinis and the Master of Happiness

by Kanya Remembrance

Once, when I was a young girl, I was driving down the freeway in Los Angeles with my father in our funky old Ford. My father asked me a question that many parents ask their children: "What do you want to be when you grow up?" I told my father, "I want to be happy."

Many years later my father reminded me of this incident. He told me then that my wish had been granted because I had been blessed to become a practitioner of the Way of the Heart. He was right. Somehow, even though I grew up in a very ordinary, Spiritually uninspired circumstance, I have been drawn by Grace to my Heart-Master, Da Love-Ananda Hridayam. For the past fourteen years I have lived in the Sphere of His Blessing and have practiced the Way of Happiness that He has Revealed.

I came to Heart-Master Da Love-Ananda when I was already nineteen years old. Since then, I have often felt that it would have been wonderful to grow up in His Company. Every day of the more than fourteen years that I have been blessed to spend as a student and devotee of Heart-Master Da Love-Ananda has been full of Blessing, and full of lessons about what it takes to be truly Happy. Heart-Master Da Love-Ananda has

Worked very diligently, very patiently, and with great Love and Divine Genius to Teach me about Happiness.

Through His Compassionate Service to me, I have come to understand how important it is to spend time in Good Company, or in the Company of One who is truly Awake and Free. This principle has been understood since ancient times in all the great religious and Spiritual traditions, and I have been very fortunate to rediscover this ancient secret in my relationship to Heart-Master Da Love-Ananda. And now you can understand something about why I would have loved to have been with Heart-Master Da Love-Ananda for my entire life.

There are four girls who have been so Blessed. Io Brahmacharini, Shawnee Brahmacharini, Naamleela Brahmacharini, and Tamarind Brahmacharini have lived and practiced in Heart-Master Da Love-Ananda's "Bright" Sphere of Divine Happiness since they were born. All their lives they have been Blessed with the great Gift of direct Instruction and Guidance from Him.

This does not mean that these girls have not encountered any struggles. Far from it. A great deal has been required of them. Heart-Master Da Love-Ananda has Taught that by birth, human beings are not disposed to be always already Happy. Instead, we look for fulfillment and Happiness through all kinds of objects or others or events in order to become Happy. But true Happiness can never be found by the one who seeks it—for you have to abandon Happiness in order to look for it. Instead, true Happiness is always already the case! That is why Heart-Master Da Love-Ananda has told us, "You cannot become Happy. You can only be Happy."

How do we discover the secret of how to be Happy? Heart-Master Da always Reveals this Happiness whenever anyone—whether it be me or the Brahmacharinis or you—practices as He suggests we do. That is the Gift that He Gives to anyone who comes into His Company. (And you can be in His Spiritual and Divine Company just by giving Him your feeling-attention, even now, as you read this book.)

Holy places—places set aside for sacred purposes because they have been blessed in one way or another—are another form of Good Company that has been honored throughout the centuries. The most powerful of holy sites are those Blessed by great Happiness-Realizers.

Over the years of His Great Heart-Work, Heart-Master Da Love-Ananda has Blessed three major Hermitage Ashrams—Sri Love-Anandashram in Fiji, Tumomama in Hawaii, and The Mountain Of Attention in northern California. All three are powerful beyond compare—you can feel His Blessing-Force pervading every inch of these holy places. Because the Brahmacharinis have lived in Heart-Master Da's Gurukula, they have always lived in these Hermitage Ashrams or Sanctuaries, where devotees have provided a residence for Him. Such Sanctuaries provide a setting where many devotees can come together and practice in Heart-Master Da Love-Ananda's Company.

Over time, He has Guided us in creating a form of life to be lived on the Sanctuaries. This form includes everything that devotees—adults and children alike—need for human and religious and Spiritual growth. It provides time each day for each individual to express his or her devotion through meditation, study, exercise, service, sacred arts, the discipline of relationship, and other daily occasions of celebration and Remembrance of Heart-Master Da Love-Ananda, Who Reveals the Divine Mystery.

As a result of their unique background and the fact that they have spent their entire lives in Heart-Master Da Love-Ananda's Good Company, Brahmacharinis Io, Shawnee, Tamarind, and Naamleela are not ordinary children. Their understanding of ordinary reality is clear. Because they have studied and practiced the Way of the Heart since birth and have always been Guided by Heart-Master Da Love-Ananda, they have an understanding of the nature and the laws of ordinary reality that is truly unique. Because their minds, and feelings, and bodily lives have been Served to turn beyond un-Happiness by His direct Heart-Wisdom, their vision (or their intuitive response to life and Happiness) is pure and unclouded by false notions. Their capacity to change and be humanly and religiously responsive is therefore uncommon. They are balanced and Happy children. I can see this just by looking at them or spending time with them. Heart-Master Da Love-Ananda's Love and Work are obvious in them. They are a Happy sign in our Ashram.

That is not to say that these girls are "angels" and are only inclined to Happiness. No. But their lives have always been focused in an ego-transcending practice. They have been Guided by Heart-Master Da Love-Ananda to discover the Divine Nature of existence, to feel the Divine Mystery, and to grow in the practice of Happiness for real. This course of learning has involved them in many tests of their capacity to respond Happily to the difficult demands of life, as well as in many extremely auspicious and happy Blessings.

In 1988, Heart-Master Da left Sri Love-Anandashram in Fiji, where He had been residing, and traveled to see practitioners in New Zealand and

California. While we were in California with Him, a very important event occurred for these young practitioners, who had not yet formally become brahmacharinis.

For all of their early years, the practice of Happiness had been served and supported in them by those around them. Now Heart-Master Da Love-Ananda asked His young devotees to make the choice to practice Happiness themselves. He also asked them, if they did choose to practice, to express their commitment by becoming formal members of His Brahmacharya Order and intensifying their practice of the Way of Happiness that He Offers.

Io, Shawnee, Tamarind, and Naamleela, along with their parents, teachers, and guides, began to "consider",[1] Guided all the while by Heart-Master Da Love-Ananda, how they could respond to His Offering and create this sacred Order. They began to study the Hindu tradition of brahmacharya. In that tradition, the transition to brahmacharya practice is regarded as a "new birth" in which the young brahmacharis now live exactly the way their brahmacharya master instructs them to live. They take up a life of stern discipline, knowing that this will give them the character and heart needed for real human and Spiritual growth. And traditional brahmacharis understood that only through honoring their relationship to the Guru and accepting His Blessing Help and the Gift of His discipline would they learn to feel God, or the Mystery.

In fact, this transition is marked by a ceremony called "Upanayana" (which, in one of the most revered and ancient of Hindu texts, is said to mean "taking charge of the student"). In it, the teacher formally takes on the new brahmacharya student by saying, "Into my will I take thy heart." It is this sacred relationship between the young brahmachari and his or her master that is the heart of brahmacharya practice.

The Upanayana ceremony, which traditionally is an initiation into the sacred ways and into the vows of practice required by the Guru, marks the time when children (generally between the ages of eight and thirteen) consecrate themselves to an intense period of Spiritual learning and preparation for adult life.

We also learned that, because it is such a time of challenge, growth, and one-pointed concentration in sacred practice, brahmacharya marks a transition from the comforts of the mother's care into the wise and protective (and more demanding) custody of the Guru, or Spiritual father.

Io, Shawnee, Tamarind, and Naamleela went through a process that reflected this traditional wisdom. But their transition was also unique to the Way that their own Heart-Master Reveals. They very Happily chose this unique brahmacharya practice in the Way of the Heart. Inspired by Heart-Master Da's Great Vision of what their lives should be, they began to let go of everything that distracted them from practice. Their desire to devote themselves to the study of God in Heart-Master Da Love-Ananda's Company was very clear and inspiring.

Since their birth, it had been everyone's hope that these girls would increasingly show the signs of great respect for Heart-Master Da Love-Ananda, real devotion to Him as Heart-Master, dedication to the disciplines He had Given them, commitment to academic studies, and proficiency in sacred arts. Now Heart-Master Da Love-Ananda acknowledged that these signs were alive in the Brahmacharinis. This was a most auspicious and happy event, and the Brahmacharinis and their families celebrated their movement into full brahmacharya life by acknowledging Heart-Master Da Love-Ananda as their Brahmacharya Master and Spiritual Father.

From this time on, the Brahmacharinis would be under His Care and Direction. It was no longer necessary for them to be "parented" in the manner necessary for younger children. They had proven through their growing maturity that they were ready for the challenges more characteristic of the third stage of life.

Under Heart-Master Da Love-Ananda's Wise Guidance, the Brahmacharinis and their parents had been going through the natural process of releasing one another as they grew older. This process is like a mother bird's carefully nudging her offspring out of the nest at just the right time, so they learn to fly on their own. Heart-Master Da now indicated that this time had come—they no longer needed to cling to their parents in a childish way. It was time for them to grow in their relationship to Heart-Master Da, to their families, and to the culture at large.

It is traditional, in preparing for the Upanayana ceremony, for the mother and the brahmacharya applicant to eat a special "last" meal together. This ritual meal means that the brahmachari is being released so that he or she can enter into the next phase of growth. Similarly, the Brahmacharinis' mothers now released them to the wonderful and demanding circumstance that Heart-Master Da was extending to them as maturing young practitioners of Happiness.

From now on, the Brahmacharinis would live with Sat-Guru Da as Heart-Master and with the Kanyas, who would serve as their intimates and guides, providing all the nurturing energy and support that they required to grow in their practice. This was a joyous event for the families involved and for the four girls.

When these young practitioners responded to Heart-Master Da Love-Ananda's Calling: "Conform to Me—My Happiness and My discipline—and live as My Brahmacharinis," they were formally initiated into the Brahmacharya Order He had established.

During their Upanayana initiation, the Brahmacharinis received white shawls that Heart-Master Da had Blessed for them to wear. He Instructed them to wear these shawls as well as their malas[2] and brahmacharya uniforms as an obvious sign to others of their commitment to brahmacharya practice.

Heart-Master Da Love-Ananda appointed the members of The Hridaya Da Gurukula Kanyadana Kumari Mandala as Spiritual guides for these Brahmacharinis, and each Brahmacharini was initiated by her Kanya intimate. Brahmacharini Shawnee describes the day of their initiation.

The Upanayana initiation in California May 4, 1988

BRAHMACHARINI SHAWNEE: On the morning of our Upanayana initiation ceremony, we heard a presentation about the ceremony and what would occur in it, what it means, and what its results would be. Then we discussed our feelings about making this commitment. I knew it meant a big change for us, and I felt very happy about this. I knew that this was the choice I wanted to make. Then we proceeded to the meditation hall for the ceremony. I felt very fortunate to be Graced with this opportunity. One at a time we were initiated at the altar. As I bowed and walked back to my seat after my initiation, I knew that I had to take more responsibility for my practice, and I wondered what effect this change would have in our lives.

Everyone, young or old, feels at heart that he or she wants to be happy, just as I did when I was driving in the car with my father. What is remarkable about these girls is that, since birth, they have been given a circumstance in which that Heart-Impulse is called to the fore. And now their Heart-Master was asking them to focus their lives entirely in that

Impulse. But, as Brahmacharini Shawnee knew on the day of their initiation, this was just the beginning. The real challenges and fruits of brahmacharya life had yet to reveal themselves.

After the ceremony, all of their brahmacharya practices were refined, and they began to apply themselves with much greater energy and attention to the daily schedule of religious study, service, physical Yogic exercises, meditation, chanting, sacramental worship, academic study, sacred arts, and other practical and relational life-disciplines. (We lived this intensified form of sadhana, or Spiritual practice, everywhere we went. After the initiation in California, we continued to travel in California and on to Hawaii, creatively finding ways to live all the practices Heart-Master Da Love-Ananda has specified in their daily schedule.) He Gave me (and all those who served the Brahmacharinis) the responsibility to maintain their complete brahmacharya schedule and discipline without fail, no matter what kind of circumstance or apparent obstacle we might confront as we traveled. We took His request seriously. Even though it was not easy and we were not always able to live the form perfectly, our commitment was such that the imperfections of any circumstance did not become a significant distraction. The Brahmacharinis were able to remain fundamentally focused in their self-transcending practice.

When we returned to Sri Love-Anandashram after seven months of traveling, the resident practitioners there did not fully understand the change that had taken place for these four young practitioners. They continued to relate to the girls as they had in the past—not requiring the degree of discipline and maturity of the Brahmacharinis that they had come up to since their initiation. I noticed that the quality of the Brahmacharinis' discipline and their energy and attention for practice in Heart-Master Da Love-Ananda's Company gradually began to dissipate. They began to animate old and un-Happy tendencies.

And that is where the story begins.

The Honey Incident

by Brahmacharini Shawnee

It was October 25, 1988, the day before Hermitage Day. Every year on this day (which we now call "Naitauba Padavara") we celebrate Heart-Master Da Love-Ananda's first arrival in 1983 at Sri Love-Anandashram, or Naitauba Island. (Naitauba Padavara celebrates Heart-Master Da's "Best" or Most Auspicious [vara] Footstep [pada] on the island of Naitauba.) Jeff Hughes, one of the Ashram gardeners, was working down at the kitchen separating a large amount of home-grown honey from the honeycomb and putting it in pots. With my companions Brahmacharini Io, Allison, and Story, I came across him (or rather the honey) while we were clearing our plates from lunch. We walked by and gave the delicious-looking honey a significant glance. We took care of our dishes and strolled casually toward a large heap of honeycomb, still gooey with the sweet substance.

We offered to relieve Jeff of some of this "excess waste product", in an offhand sort of way, as if we ate honey every day and could take it or leave it at will (whereas, in fact, I have had a "no honey" discipline for many years because I always have very negative reactions to sweets—no matter how good they taste in the moment!)

Jeff, unaware of this discipline or of how honey affects me, magnanimously offered us as much as we cared to eat. We ransacked the bowl, enthusiastically grabbing at the honey-coated honeycomb as if we were just fulfilling the law of gravitation. Then we ran off with our loot, eyes glowing with eager anticipation. We savored each lick, but it all ended too soon, and eventually the honey was gone. "Let's go get some more!" Brahmacharini Io suggested devilishly.

We all were quick to agree, and it wasn't long before we were gathered around the large bowl, making hinting remarks, "Gosh, it sure looks good, ummmm! What does it taste like?" And finally some not-so-hinting remarks like, "Can we have some?" Again Jeff generously offered us the honeycomb in all its abundance. We each liberally snatched at the delicacy and were about to take flight when a surprised voice stopped us.

"What are you girls doing?" Lynne Closser, our teacher and intimate of many years, had suddenly and unexpectedly appeared on the scene. Brahmacharini Io and I turned and high-tailed it out of there, leaving our plunder in the wondering hands of Allison and Story, who didn't seem to see any misbehavior in the theft. We put as much

distance as we could between us and Lynne before she stopped us in our tracks with a loud shout.

Lynne came over to us, told us how disappointed she was with us, and asked us, in an almost disbelieving tone of voice, why we were going against our disciplines. I knew

---

what I had done was wrong. (But I really didn't see why we couldn't just conveniently "forget" about the discipline every once in a while. Really, I was struggling with the practice, and as you can see, even took advantage of opportunities to avoid the discipline.) I listened with only mild interest until Lynne declared that she was going to suggest to Kanya Remembrance that we refrain from having sweets on the following day. Since tomorrow we were to celebrate Hermitage Day and a very special meal (including dessert and treats) had been planned, this was serious. I knew only too well that when Lynne suggests something to Kanya Remembrance, whatever she suggests usually comes to pass, for Kanya Remembrance will take no nonsense (and for good reason). That evening when we were called to come to the Kanyas' residence, The Giver Of Joy, to receive Notes[1] from Heart-Master Da Love-Ananda, we knew that we had taken the matter all too lightly.

Brahmacharini Io and I tried to forget about the incident and our impending consequence and we hoped that Lynne would, too. However, our misbehavior did not escape from her memory or from the ears of Kanya Remembrance.

Lynne Closser with the Brahmacharinis

Life Is like a Golf Course

You Have to Hit the Ball Straight down the Center!

by Kanya Remembrance

When Lynne told me that the Brahmacharinis had eaten the honey, she and I discussed what our response would be. Over the years, we have become very aware of the importance of maintaining a right diet. We have noticed that when children eat certain foods, particularly sweets, they are thrown out of balance. They become dull, irritable, easily distracted, and even reactive. Right diet is key to preparing a base of full and balanced energy and attention for our life of practice. Particularly in Brahmacharini Shawnee's case, any form of excessive sweetness causes her to be overly emotional and drained of energy (after the surge of energy she gets from the sweet). Because this is so, honey is not a regular part of the Brahmacharinis' diet. Brahmacharini Shawnee (and the other Brahmacharinis) know that they have such sweets only when treats are offered at a special celebration and that even then they only have as much as they can handle. But since their lives around Heart-Master Da Love-Ananda are always full of delight, and He finds so many ways to surround them with His Humor and Love, they are not deprived in any way because we ask them not to eat honey.

It became clear to me that not only were the adults in the Ashram not well enough informed about the Brahmacharinis' new practice to be able to rightly serve them, but that the girls themselves were not wholly committed to the brahmacharya discipline. It was their lack of wholehearted commitment, and not so much the fact that they had taken a little honey, that motivated me to take action. I felt that we needed to take a dramatic step in our service to the girls.

As Heart-Master Da Love-Ananda is their Brahmacharya Master, He is always informed of any significant developments in their practice. When I told Him about this incident and the discipline of no sweets on Hermitage Day, which I thought would be an appropriate consequence, I thought He might feel I was being too strict. (Heart-Master Da Love-Ananda has always Guided me in my service to the girls and has teased me many times about being too strict with them!) After I finished, He sat silently for a few moments. Then He leaned forward and said, "There should be more discipline than that."

When, to my surprise, He responded this way, I knew that He was choosing to use this incident to "grow" the Brahmacharinis by creating a lesson out of it that would serve their self-transcending practice. He told me to cancel the special breakfast that the Brahmacharinis and the Kanyas were to have with Him on the morning of Hermitage Day. He also said that for the Brahmacharinis who broke the discipline, desserts were to be eliminated for at least a month (desserts in the Ashram being of a most humble variety). They would have no cake on Heart-Master Da's Birthday, and there would be no reading of novels and fantasy books and story books that are not serious, useful, instructive literature. He said that, for the next month, those evenings normally spent with their intimates should instead be given over to additional religious instruction. He said that Brahmacharinis need the influence of people who live a strict renunciate discipline and who will oblige and hold them to the discipline. People had not been serious enough about their own practice, and thus the children did not feel obliged to practice the Ashram discipline.

He then went on to speak about how this incident reflected on many aspects of the Brahmacharinis' practice, and their need for a greater understanding of the vow they had taken. He outlined a number of changes that needed to be made. Because Halloween was coming up and because we had, in the past, celebrated it in the usual manner, one of the changes was how we were to conduct our Halloween celebration now and in the future. This is what He said:

HEART-MASTER DA LOVE-ANANDA: Since our return to Sri Love-Anandashram, the Brahmacharinis have spent too much time with people who are not their formal guides, and they have frequently been allowed to abandon their discipline. I have made it clear to you that the Kanyas are responsible for these children. You are their guides. Their initiation was not merely a ritual. It was real. We have to find a way to concentrate them in their relationships with their Kanya guides. And you Kanyas must maintain your responsibilities in relationship to the children. Where do you think the children get this point of view that they do not have to live the brahmacharya discipline without fail?

KANYA REMEMBRANCE: I feel they have not been guided consistently and sufficiently to keep to the discipline.

HEART-MASTER DA LOVE-ANANDA: You should learn from this incident. Make sure that everyone who associates with the children is oriented to relate to them appropriately. You must take a look at all the influences in their lives.

The Brahmacharinis should not be around conventional, self-indulgent people who do not live the discipline of self-transcendence. Such people are always creating some excuse to abandon their own discipline or to interrupt the sequence of the brahmacharya discipline. The people who serve the children must themselves demonstrate a commitment to discipline. They must be able to help the children maintain the discipline through the force of their own practice, their own example. The children must have guides who can inspire them and help them maintain their brahmacharya discipline absolutely. They must help them to make use of their time for the sake of their practice of the Way of the Heart. The adult guides must create a presence that keeps the children's egos from dominating them and doing their own thing.

An example of the undisciplined, conventional orientation can be found in the way celebrations are conducted. In our time and place, celebrations that were traditionally religious have become middle-class holidays. Who thinks about what the sacred nature of any celebration really is? All the celebrations of practitioners of the Way of the Heart should become true religious celebrations based on the Wisdom of the Way of the Heart.

In fact, we should cancel our conventional celebration of Halloween. What am I going to do on Halloween—go out and put on a mask? I have done that. I have had to conform to your way of celebrating. Now all of our celebrations should conform to Me. I am not going to be like you anymore. You should be like Me.[1]

Conventionally, Halloween is all about getting sweets. The "honey incident" is just an example of where that orientation leads. Showering children with sweets is just a way of diverting their energy and encouraging them to indulge in eating junk.

It was obvious to me that He was describing the very thing that had happened. It made complete sense—because the adults had taught them to eat sweets at this time of year, they felt free to indulge in the honey even though they knew they should not ordinarily.

Heart-Master Da continued His Instruction:

HEART-MASTER DA LOVE-ANANDA: From now on, in our culture, Halloween will be a day of purification. We will transform that day by giving it a religious orientation. (Sat-Guru Da sat quietly for a moment before He continued to Give His Blessing-Instruction on how to serve the Brahmacharinis.)

You must have a clear notion of what each individual girl values and how the withdrawal of a privilege will affect each one.

KANYA REMEMBRANCE: We do have their disciplines outlined in the brahmacharya manual.

HEART-MASTER DA LOVE-ANANDA: No. It is a very subtle matter. I had to fully "consider" precisely what the appropriate discipline would be in response to the "honey incident". I had to carefully "consider" what would affect each girl, so that each one would be served very specifically. At their age, you must deal with them through social discipline, so they can see that there are real consequences when they violate a discipline. You must know each child so precisely that you know exactly what to withdraw if she violates the discipline. You must apply the discipline with subtlety.

The Brahmacharinis are to live the discipline, and that is it. Their life is a life in God. It is a God-Realizing life. They are not here to be middle-class householders. They are here to live the discipline and to be accountable to Me.

What they have been showing us lately simply cannot be tolerated.

One day when we were in Hawaii, I walked through a golf course at a large hotel. I stood up on a hill and looked down at the golf course. A fairway led right to the hole in front of Me. On one side of the fairway there was a water hazard, and on the other side there was a sand trap. That scene is a vision of what life is like.

You must keep to the center to reach the hole. If you look to the right, if you look to the left, if you go either way, you fall into a trap.

Life is also like this. Life creates traps. If you do not live the discipline of attention, you fall into the trap. The discipline of attention helps you to maintain your direction straight ahead. Therefore, to strictly maintain the discipline of attention is the law. If you do not maintain the discipline, you fall into the trap. Such is the nature of life. Either it rewards you or else you fall into the trap. The reward is that you stay aligned to the Center, or the Divine Being, and you Realize the Truth. But if you do not live the discipline, then you fall to either side and you are caught in the trap.

That is exactly what life is like—and the traps are always there. Life is a system that rewards straightness and penalizes diversions to the left or the right. If you indulge in diversions and live as if there are no penalties, you will grow up to be a silly adult, and you will get straightened out only with a great deal of difficulty, because your mind will be confused.

You must teach the children what the diversions are about. You must let the children know that this is not a heavenly realm, and that they have to keep straight. If they think they can get away with not living the discipline, you must show them the traps. Life itself will not always show the traps immediately, and the traps may not be obvious. Therefore, if you do not show the children the traps, they will get caught in the illusion that if something appears to be positive, it is not a trap.

If they do not maintain the discipline, then you must show the traps to them. And discipline is the method for showing children the traps. If they do not live the discipline, they will get caught in illusions. Therefore, when they grow up, their minds will be confused, and they will have to go through a great ordeal of difficulty to get straightened out.

Those who have contact with the Brahmacharinis do not understand this. They do not have this point of view yet. The adults themselves do not understand this lesson of life, and, therefore, they have not maintained the discipline themselves. They have just been indulging themselves in My Company and not living the Way of the Heart. They therefore think the traps do not exist. They do not know that life rewards straightness and that in the diversions there are traps. That is why the children have not been raised rightly. The adults must understand this, and the Brahmacharinis also.

That is why, in the traditions, brahmacharis and tulkus are always accountable to religious teachers who understand and are always demonstrating this example. That is why the traditional discipline is so strict. Traditionally, if you move an inch to one side or the other, you get the stick immediately. You are required to maintain the discipline without fail. This is also how to guide the children and keep them straight. You must make sure that this is done.

It was clear that we needed to help the Brahmacharinis become concentrated in their practice. We changed their daily schedule so that they could spend more time with the Kanyas and less time with others not so prepared to serve their brahmacharya practice. Heart-Master Da also suggested that the treats the girls had been looking forward to receiving on Halloween be given to the residents of the neighboring Fijian village. He further suggested that the girls themselves take the sweets to the village and distribute the candies to the Fijian villagers, who would still be observing Halloween in the usual manner.

Halloween at Ciqomi

by Brahmacharini Shawnee

T he next day we did exactly that. Carrying two trays heavily laden with sweets of many varieties, we boarded the white Land Rover at about three o'clock. There were carob leaves, carob treats filled with caramel, jelly, fruit, and honey, popcorn balls, big sweets, little sweets, sweets of all shapes and colors. Both trays were heaped with mountains of treats. We crowded into the small truck and undertook the uncomfortable journey over the hill to the Fijian village of Ciqomi (pronounced "Thing-GO-mee").

As we rounded the last corner, a familiar sight met our eyes. Many of the Fijian villagers were out on their porches talking or relaxing. The driver parked the car and we piled out onto the warm grass. Then we meandered down to the first house.

At each house we told the Fijians that these sweets were from Dau Loloma (which is Heart-Master Da Love-Ananda's Fijian Name). They knew and we knew that these sweets were not just something that tasted

good—they were a form of His Blessing for the Fijians. We gave each person three or four sweets and continued to the next house. Everyone was eager to receive the candy. Finally we had completed our circle of the village. We looked at the trays. They were only half empty! We stood outside the meeting bure (BOO-ray), which is the large building with a thatched roof at the center of their village, and called everyone who wanted more sweets to come down to us. Soon we were enveloped in a swarm of children. We filled their hands till they overflowed. Then they wandered away. We still had more sweets to give out, so we looked in the meeting bure. A large assembly of Fijian men were sitting quietly. We asked who wanted more. A loud rumbling filled our ears as the men rose to their feet. In a moment the room became a mass of waving hands.

One man would hold out his hand, get a sweet, put it behind his back and pretend he had not gotten any yet. It was all we could do to fill the many open hands. Finally everyone sat down again. There were two sweets left. We asked, "Who didn't get enough?" Two men jumped up, bumping each other as they ran trying to get the last two. We all laughed!

The ordeal of giving up Halloween was over. The trays were empty, and we walked back to the car. We knew that this had been a good and even necessary thing for us to do, because we felt far happier at having given away all the sweets than we ever would have been in eating them!

Guru and God Twenty-Four Hours a Day

by Kanya Remembrance

After this, the Brahmacharinis' energy and attention became much more focused in their Given discipline, and in general, they began to show a greater commitment to practice. As is the case with all forms of discipline, there is a level of frustration and difficulty (traditionally called "tapas", or "heat") that arises when you are disciplining the tendencies of the ego. This was certainly the case for the Brahmacharinis. They felt the bite of applying themselves more fiercely than before to the discipline their Heart-Master was requiring of them for the sake of Happiness. On the one hand, they responded very positively to these changes, and yet, on the other hand, they continued in various instances to dramatize their old habits of resistance and indulgence. On one occasion, two of the Brahmacharinis got into conflict with one another.

As I accompanied Heart-Master Da Love-Ananda on a walk one day, I described to Him my observations of the Brahmacharinis' response to their discipline. I mentioned that Brahmacharini Shawnee, in particular, needed to have a more refined discipline relative to her emotional character, and I described a few circumstances in which the Brahmacharinis had created conflicts with one another.

I told Heart-Master Da that I had noticed Brahmacharini Shawnee in particular had been involved in creating conflicts with the other

Brahmacharinis. In general, she seemed to be more loving to animals than to other people! Because of this I suggested to Heart-Master Da that perhaps she should no longer have her daily period of serving and riding horses until she was willing to bring that same sensitivity to other people.

Heart-Master Da Love-Ananda then Instructed me by telling me that we should not interrupt her participation with the horses, as this was her sacred art and a formal program of study she had a responsibility to maintain and develop. He let me know that when a consequence is required for a member of the Brahmacharya Order, the discipline of the daily schedule should not be interrupted, but (instead) more responsibilities should be added to the daily activities. This is what He said:

HEART-MASTER DA LOVE-ANANDA: What you have been doing obviously has not been effective, because Shawnee is not taking us seriously enough. Part of the Brahmacharinis' discipline is that they are to be observed and they must maintain their discipline at all times.

How is it that Shawnee was able to get into conflict with another Brahmacharini? Someone should have been there with them. The brahmacharya discipline should be such that they never have the space to indulge these dramatizations. We should not have to take a great deal of time to creatively decide what is appropriate discipline every time a child dramatizes her egoic tendencies. The daily form of their schedule, in and of itself, should be the discipline. And the form should allow them no space for dramatizing.

For example, when Shawnee dramatizes as she just has, we should not have to decide what she will or will not do as a consequence. She should know that if she is observed to be dramatizing she must return to her discipline immediately. Then for the rest of the day, all she is given to do is her discipline. That is the way the Brahmacharinis are to live. Their life is about discipline.

KANYA REMEMBRANCE: The conventional notion is that we must give children "space" in order for them to grow. Many people seem to feel that we cannot always be observing children, and that we have to give them space in which to be creative.

HEART-MASTER DA LOVE-ANANDA: That is a wrong point of view. The human space that you should give children is in the context of relationship. But children who are brahmacharis are always to be kept accountable. They are to be observed always. The farthest you should get from them is to give them enough space to, perhaps, play on the lawn while you are watching them. They are to be observed twenty-four hours a day.

Of course, this is the brahmacharya discipline. If someone does not choose to live in Ashram, then perhaps the brahmacharya discipline does not apply (at least in the strictest sense). But once you have committed yourself to living the circumstance of Ashram as a brahmachari, there are certain disciplines that you must observe.

The reason the Brahmacharinis must be observed twenty-four hours a day and kept accountable is that we are trying to develop in them a life of self-transcendence rather than self-fulfillment. It is an illusion to feel that if you give a child space, his or her Divine Nature will manifest. If you give a child space, his or her egoity will manifest. Children must be held accountable and kept strictly to the discipline by constant observation and constant service to their practice.

It is important that they come to value this discipline. If they do not, then they will only embrace the discipline because "mommy" or "daddy" says to. In other words, they will develop an inappropriate relationship to the discipline—they will just be doing it because of the feeling of the demand or the threat.

They must begin to feel that living the discipline is the circumstance of Happiness. In other words, Happiness is evoked in the midst of sadhana. A mature practitioner can evoke and inspire that feeling in children. Then children (so inspired) will begin to value sadhana. The other reason they must begin to value and want to live the discipline is that if they practice just because "mommy" and "daddy" say to, they will create a secret life.

KANYA REMEMBRANCE: This is what Brahmacharini Shawnee has been doing. She appears to be practicing when she is in front of people who she feels expect that of her. But then she has a secret life where she creates a little club with other children and adults to avoid discipline and get away with whatever she can.

HEART-MASTER DA LOVE-ANANDA: All of you lived secretly when you were young. You doubted everything that was sacred and you lived an egoic life. This double life that the children have begun to live has to do

The Hridaya Da Gurukula Brahmacharini Mandala with Heart-Master Da

with the ordinary company they have kept since they were young. Children observe the adults who pretend to make the demand for discipline on them, and they also observe that these adults do not live the discipline themselves. They see the adults play phony games, and this encourages them to lead a double life also.

The only adults who can oblige the children to live the discipline are those who also live the discipline themselves and who do not live a phony life. Phony adult practitioners must not serve the children. Those who serve the Brahmacharinis must be people who command respect. Only such mature practitioners can inculcate in the Brahmacharinis an understanding of the necessity to be straight and real. Otherwise, the children feel that discipline is nonsense.

The Brahmacharinis are special children in the sense that they are being brought up under My tutelage as their Heart-Teacher and Sat-Guru. Therefore, they are being required to live a strict brahmacharya life. I want to be able to establish this brahmacharya practice once and for all in the real and traditional fashion, but in the manner of the Way of the Heart. We must make this very clear to the children.

In traditional Tibetan culture, certain children are chosen as tulkus. Similarly, our Brahmacharinis have been chosen, by virtue of their special relationship to Me, to live this very strict traditional discipline. I expect this of them. They are to be called to the form of the discipline in every moment. And that is it. Never accept any conflict whatsoever.

For example, the boys at the Ashram of Swami Prakashananda,[1] who was a brahmacharya schoolmaster, demonstrate an exemplary form of adherence to this traditional discipline. You should study such traditions to see what I mean by the order and the form that I expect these girls to maintain.

There are to be no spaces where the children are not obliged to practice. Everyone has the tendency to transform all of life to the preferences of egoity. This is true everywhere in the community of practitioners and also with the Brahmacharinis. I have Given everything required for this Way of life, but people tend to transform whatever I Give into a way of preserving and glorifying

Swami
Prakashananda

their egoity, rather than using and maintaining what I Give in a sacred manner. Everyone is always tending to destroy the Sacred.

I do not want these children to be brought up as egos. Their life must be purposed for the sake of Liberation. The children's innate egoity comes out all the time if you do not redirect them. There is no innate Divinity that can come out if they are left on their own.

The Brahmacharinis must become really Divinely oriented. Their Happiness must come from doing sadhana, and they must be very orderly people, living an orderly life twenty-four hours a day, with no free spaces. The form and schedule of their life is the discipline. They should be Happy and expressive in relationship, but always within the context of discipline. Their focus must be Guru and God twenty-four hours a day.

Heart-Master Da Grants His Blessing to His devotees

"Holy Mackerel! I Did It Again!"

by Brahmacharini Shawnee

I have (or rather had) the responsibility of feeding the cats every morning, because I have an interest in animals. On one particular day I went out to feed the cats. They have a diet of a cold grain—rice or millet—and some chunks of canned mackerel, and various vegetables are added to the mixture, too. This combination is delicious to the cats, but it would normally be a revolting meal to me. However, on this particular day when I fed the cats, I thought, "How good it looks!" and without a moment's hesitation I snatched a handful of their food, finished my service, and headed toward No Doubt Of God, our brahmacharya residence, munching on my handful of stolen mackerel rice. No sooner had I rounded the corner than I came face to face with Kanya Remembrance.

No Doubt Of God

"What are you eating, Brahmacharini Shawnee?" she asked me, knowing that I have been asked to exhibit the good manners of eating only while seated at the table. I quickly put my hand (full of cat food) behind my back and stealthily dropped its contents on the ground, putting my foot over the lump. But Kanya Remembrance has strong eyes and she saw it. This time I gave myself up for lost. I knew that I had dramatized in an exaggerated way and that there would be real consequences.

KANYA REMEMBRANCE: It was not so much that eating the cat food was such a terrible thing to do. Of course, Brahmacharini Shawnee is a practicing vegetarian and she has chosen to live the dietary discipline of this Way of life, and mackerel cat food is definitely not part of that diet, no matter how many vegetables or grains are added to it! But what was more important was the statement Brahmacharini Shawnee was making about her participation in the practice altogether. She was demonstrating a disposition of greater and greater resistance to the magnified demand to live the Ashram life.

Brahmacharini Shawnee is a very strong-willed character and a natural leader. Often these qualities are a great asset, but now she was animating them in a way that was disturbing—both to her and to others. Now I watched as Heart-Master Da did exactly what He had Instructed me to do earlier. He was very sensitive to Brahmacharini Shawnee's particular character in providing her discipline. Because of His profound intimacy with her, Heart-Master Da Love-Ananda's response was a strong one. He knew exactly how to help her make a clear choice. He asked that I gather the Brahmacharinis and all the Kanyas together so that I could pass on His response to the "mackerel incident" and what it represented for Brahmacharini Shawnee.

HEART-MASTER DA LOVE-ANANDA: *Tell Shawnee she has dishonored the Brahmacharya Order. She has dishonored her relationship to Me and refused My discipline, and she has been doing things secretly. So we should have a formal ceremony of disciplining her participation in the Brahmacharya Order. We should take her mala and her shawl from her and we should make it very clear to her why we are doing this. She should move out of No Doubt Of God and live in the Hermitage village under the supervision of the village culture.*

She should live in a simple circumstance with no amusements. She should have nothing to do with animals. She should not watch any television but should simply study and serve. She should never be left on her own. She should have nothing to do with the other Brahmacharinis or the Kanyas. She should do her schooling alone and serve among adults. She should continue religious studies every day, but she should not be involved in any devotional or religious practices, because she has not honored her relationship to Me. She should not come to see Me until she demonstrates a right relationship to Me as her Sat-Guru.

Her circumstance will not change until she again earns her active participation in the Brahmacharya Order. And I do not mean just making a few signs here or there over the next few days. She really must prove that she no longer has a secret life, and she must show that she wants to live a brahmacharya life. If she does not want to, then she can continue to live in this circumstance in the village.

You, Remembrance, should have a real conversation with her about her life and practice. Ask her if she wants to live here and practice the brahmacharya discipline. Does she really want to do this? She must let us know if she really wants to live the Way of the Heart. She does not have to if she does not want to. But if she does, she must demonstrate that she really wants to live the life of a brahmacharya practitioner. If she does not want to live this Way of life, what does she want to do instead? Does she want to go to a public school, or does she want to live here and practice in My Company?

If she does want to be in My Company, she will have to actually practice this Way of life. If she does want to practice, she should live in the circumstance that I have described until she demonstrates a change. She must be obedient to Me and to the other adults here as well. If she wants to act like an adolescent, she will have to do this somewhere else, because it is not appropriate for her to live in an Ashram and continue to dramatize an egoic, adolescent life. She must live here based on her own real choice, and she must live the Way of the Heart as a true Brahmacharini. All of the Brahmacharinis must understand this and know that their dramatizations will not be tolerated either.

KANYA REMEMBRANCE: After we had heard Heart-Master Da Love-Ananda's Instructions and His questions about Brahmacharini Shawnee's commitment to this Way of life, we all talked with her. She told us that she did want to stay and practice. But she did not say it with any kind of conviction or energy. She just shook her head or nodded to indicate yes or no. She was hanging on to her emotional disturbance and not practicing self-transcending Happiness during our conversation.

When I served Heart-Master Da Love-Ananda's dinner, I told Him about my conversation with Brahmacharini Shawnee. She had told me that she wanted to stay and practice and that she did not want to go away or be anywhere else. He questioned me about the energy she brought to this confession. Even though I very much wanted her to have made a full response to her Heart-Master, I had to be honest. When He heard that she had only nodded her response, He replied:

HEART-MASTER DA LOVE-ANANDA: I cannot trust her confession unless she begins to practice immediately. And the first evidence that she is practicing is that she must talk about what she is feeling and what she has been trying to communicate by refusing to practice.

Shawnee goes through a ceremony of saying she wants to practice, but in the moment of the daily demand to practice, she does not do it. I am not interested in letting her continue this ceremony of confessing and then creating further disturbance to Ashram life. Anybody who lives here in this Ashram, including the Brahmacharinis, must meet the demand of Ashram discipline. If Shawnee continues in her present mood, she will just be a burden in the village and not a happy participant in the culture of practice. She must show us she is actually choosing to practice by talking about what she is really feeling. It is necessary for her to do this so that she can understand herself. Then she will really be able to practice in relationship to Me and to others.

Shawnee's Confession

by Kanya Remembrance

T hat evening I met with Brahmacharini Shawnee and, even though it was a very emotional ordeal for her, she was able to talk about what she had been feeling. This is what she confessed to me:

BRAHMACHARINI SHAWNEE: For a long time, I have not been able to feel the Mystery. I have been having a hard time trying to meditate since I was eight years old, and it gets harder as I grow older.

I have thought about this every day for a long time, but I have been afraid to tell anyone. I got so frustrated that I felt I would never be able to meditate again, and this has made me sad.

I have not been able to feel the Mystery strongly for a very long time. I have only felt the Mystery really strongly twice in the past five years. I was afraid to confess this, because I thought that people would be upset with me.

Particularly in the past few weeks when the discipline and the demand to practice has become stronger and stronger, I became more and more frustrated and mad. I stopped trying because I felt I was not going to be able to do it. I just gave up. What I was trying to say by doing these rebellious things is that I want help. I do want to be able to meditate, but at times I also want to be able to do what I want. I often compare myself with the other Brahmacharinis and get into conflict with them. I make negative judgments about them and their practice a lot.

Also, I do not always agree with my disciplines. Sometimes I feel I am "picked on" and get more disciplines than the other girls, and then I think I must be crazy and I wish I had been born like a "normal" person.

I also notice I see things two ways. Sometimes I view things only in part, but sometimes I see things as a whole. When I see things only in part, I do not really see what I am doing, like when I dramatized by eating cat food this morning. But when I see things as a whole, it makes me more balanced. For the first time I feel unjustified in what I have done. I can see that I chose to dramatize and that I cannot blame anyone else for it.

Most of the time I am glad that I have the specific sadhana that has been Given me, and I have an intuition that a really strict life would help me to meditate and feel the Mystery. Strong disciplines have had a positive and balancing effect on me in the past.

I feel relieved at getting these things out in the open, but also scared at what Heart-Master Da Love-Ananda might say to my confession. I am in a very vulnerable position, and I am not sure I like it.

As Shawnee spoke, she visibly brightened. It was as though a great weight were being lifted from her. Heart-Master Da Love-Ananda's request that she make this confession was clearly initiating a new moment of growth in practice for her.

The Two Secrets

A Talk by The World-Teacher, Heart-Master Da Love-Ananda

K ANYA REMEMBRANCE: Even though it was late in the evening, I knew that Heart-Master Da Love-Ananda would be waiting to hear Shawnee's response. I quickly went to His room to convey all that Shawnee had confessed. I offered a flower and sat on the floor near His bed. Another one of the Kanyas was massaging His Feet, and He nodded "Yes" when I asked Him if He would like to hear my report. He listened quietly as I recounted Shawnee's confession, and then He Gave the following Instructions:

HEART-MASTER DA LOVE-ANANDA: Shawnee's main problem is that she does not want to do what she is told to do. That is it. She is now almost thirteen and entering into the process of the third stage of life. She cannot think in terms of little-kid stuff anymore. The extent of her understanding cannot just be "feeling the Mystery". She is still being instructed as if she were in the second stage of life, and this is not appropriate.

She has an emotional, and therefore a Spiritual, problem that has not been addressed rightly, that has not been dealt with in real terms. The religious life of these children has not been made real for them. They must apply themselves to a very serious and realistic study of the Way of the Heart and of life itself. They must truly learn the Way of the Heart, which is the same Wisdom and the same Process whether you are five years old or seventy.

To teach children the Way of the Heart when they are very young, it may be necessary to use concepts that relate to their early life, but the Way of the Heart itself is the same, no matter what the age of the practitioner. Therefore, you cannot reduce My Wisdom-Teaching to Sunday-school pictures. Your instruction to children must be much more serious. Their practice must be based on the same process of self-understanding that adults must realize. Children must embrace devotion, service, self-discipline, and meditation, and they must feel beyond their limits while engaging that practice.

Shawnee is not feeling the Mystery because she is not practicing devotion, service, self-discipline, and meditation. She is avoiding all of these forms of response to Me. She becomes independent and tries to think through everything. She hides her emotion and tries strategically to win a victory in her own mind. She does not do what she is told (which is to practice devotion, service, self-discipline, and meditation). She must apply herself to learning about and really practicing devotion, service, self-discipline, and meditation.

"Happiness" and "the Mystery" are meaningful words and concepts to use with children, because they are simple to grasp while children learn self-transcending devotion, service, self-discipline, and meditation. But you should not talk to them about the Mystery if you do not also talk about self-understanding and self-transcendence through devotion, service, self-discipline, and meditation. No one can just experience the Mystery and Happiness through thinking, as if you can simply think about the Mystery and Happiness and—zap!—you feel the Mystery. No. You must transcend your egoic self to feel the Mystery and to feel Happiness.

Shawnee must <u>observe</u> that she is the self-contraction. Of course she <u>is</u> the self-contraction. However, people generally do not understand this about themselves. They are full of desires and thoughts and problems and fears. And they think that they can find Happiness by seeking all the time, as if they will feel Happy when things go the way they want them to. They think that in order to be Happy, they must satisfy their desires. So they spend their time thinking, reacting, desiring, fearing, and struggling to satisfy some impulse.

And, every now and then, they feel a little Happiness. But they do not feel Happiness because it is in what they were seeking. By getting what they were seeking, for a moment they are free of seeking, because they got what they wanted. They are free of desire for the moment. For that moment they are not contracting, and because they are not contracting and are not seeking, they feel the Mystery and they are Happy. But their realization of Happiness is over very quickly.

Desire is contraction. Being afraid is contraction. Thinking is contraction. Every now and then you may be released from your search by obtaining something that you sought. But such release is actually very rare. Most people feel this Happiness for only a very few moments in an entire lifetime. You may enjoy other middling moments of pleasure, depending upon how healthy you are, but real Happiness is very rare.

Every now and then, however, someone appears as a God-Realizer Who has Realized that Happiness is already the case. He is Blissful, and He Transmits His Realization to others.

I do not just say "Be Happy" or "Feel the Mystery". You do not get to feel It by My telling you such things. Only through self-transcendence and devotion, service, self-discipline, and meditation do you get to feel It—not just through thinking about it.

The children must find out that they are contracting all the time. Children feel fear just as much as anyone else does. Even I, as a growing child, did not "feel the Mystery" all the time, after I had fully Submitted to the psycho-physical limitations of My born-condition. The Mystery is Prior Realization. Only Realization is Prior to the self-contraction. You must transcend body, emotion, thinking, and desire, and you must transcend fear. All of these things must be transcended to feel the Mystery, and these are exactly all the things that Shawnee said she has been feeling. She has been doing all of these things rather than doing what she has been told to do, which is to practice self-transcendence and devotion, service, self-discipline, and meditation. She does not feel the Mystery, because she has not been practicing devotion, service, self-discipline, and meditation. She has only been wrapped up in her fear, her desire, and her thinking.

It is good that she has found this out. To discover this is how someone becomes a real practitioner of the Way of the Heart. Just to say "Feel the Mystery" is nonsense if there is not this self-understanding. I have Revealed the Way of Understanding. You must understand and transcend your egoic self to feel the Mystery and Happiness. The Mystery, Happiness, and the Divine are always already the case. But you contract, and this keeps you from experiencing what is always already the case. Instead of feeling Happiness, the Mystery, and God, you think and fear and react and desire. Therefore, basically you just feel frustrated and afraid, and you try to get Happiness by doing all kinds of nonsensical things.

I am here to Help you to Realize God, Happiness, the Love-Bliss that is always already the case. I actually have the Power to Transmit this Realization to you, and to all beings.[1] But you must practice devotion, service, self-discipline, and meditation in relation to Me to receive My Gift.

Shawnee, and all the children, must observe that the adults are not always walking around moved by and feeling the Mystery and God all the time, because by tendency they are thinking and reacting and being afraid and seeking. All My devotees must do the sadhana of the Way of the Heart, which is devotion, service, self-discipline, meditation, and self-transcendence.

If you are able to do this, then you will receive My Spiritual Blessing more and more deeply over time. But to do this practice is work. It is an ordeal. It does not happen automatically just because you think about it. By practicing devotion to Me, by practicing feeling-Contemplation of My bodily (human) Form and My Spiritual (and Always Blessing) Presence and My Very (and Inherently Perfect) State,[2] and by practicing all the self-disciplines I recommend, people become purified of their reactivity, their desiring, their fearing, and their seeking. And to the degree that they can receive My Transmission of Love-Bliss or God or Happiness Itself, they are purified more and more of the self-contraction, and they Realize this Happiness more often and more profoundly over time. Ultimately, they may Realize God Perfectly. By doing this practice, they may realize improved conditions after death also, even higher worlds, even the Perfectly Spiritual State, depending upon how profoundly they have done sadhana and received My Gifts.

Therefore, it is up to each individual whether or not to practice the Way of the Heart that I have Revealed and do what I ask them to do.

And Shawnee must do what I ask her to do in relationship to Me, which is to practice self-transcending devotion, service, self-discipline, and meditation. Or she can refuse to practice, and she will then contract, think, react, desire, seek, and be afraid. This is mainly what she has been doing. This is your habit if you are not doing devotion, service, self-discipline, and meditation. And this is why Shawnee does not feel the Mystery, Happiness, or God. She must understand herself, then, to this degree. Either contract or else be Happy through practicing self-transcending devotion, service, self-discipline, and meditation in relation to Me. Once you become a devotee of Mine, you are faced in every moment with these two options.

As soon as Shawnee starts feeling desire, thoughts, reactivity, seeking, and fear, she should notice that she is <u>actively</u> feeling un-Happy, and that, in doing so, she cannot feel the Mystery or meditate. She did not want to tell anyone this, because she thinks that, as a practitioner, she should feel Happiness all the time.

She thinks that if she does not say the words, then she is not telling anyone that she is being the ego and not practicing. But actually she is telling everyone this all the time by what she is doing. By reacting, and by not talking about what she is feeling, and by doing secret things, she is telling us that she wants to be found out. It is a childish way of telling everyone, through her actions rather than through conversation.

She must grow up. She has no right to her childish techniques of communication anymore. She has to practice and communicate in a more and more adult way. She must be able to discuss her life and practice with her guides and with Me.

Life is difficult for all practitioners, because they are always dealing with their automatic tendencies to contract. But they must be able to communicate about these life-realities and point one another to Me and to My Wisdom-Teaching. No matter how difficult it is, they must always notice that it is their own contraction making them un-Happy, making them forget the Divine. The way to be free of this contraction is to practice self-transcending devotion, service, self-discipline, and meditation in relationship to Me, the True Heart-Master.

Children must therefore understand themselves, and they must accept the practice of devotion, service, self-transcending discipline, and meditation in relation to Me. This is how they feel beyond their contraction and are purified of the things that enforce the self-contraction and how they are able to Realize the Divine Happiness.

Children can understand this. It is the same Wisdom-Teaching that I have Given to adults. Like adult practitioners of the Way of the Heart, children should also study *The Love-Ananda Gita*.3 My Wisdom-Teaching is the same for everyone, whether they are five years old or of adult age. It is the same for all.

The Love-Ananda Gita is not complicated. I Call Shawnee to do the practice described in *The Love-Ananda Gita*, not just to feel the Mystery and be Happy. You cannot just feel the Mystery and be Happy. You must be drawn into it by going beyond your separate self. You cannot feel the Mystery by acting like you are meditating. You must really feel the Mystery.

How can you do this? You must transcend your separate and separative self. How can you do this? By practicing devotion to Me as your True Heart-Master, by serving Me as your True Heart-Master, by living all the self-disciplines that I Give to you as your True Heart-Master, and by meditating on or Contemplating Me with feeling. Therefore, you must practice devotion and service and self-discipline and feeling-Contemplation of Me, according to My Instructions. You must respect and honor My Instructions and seriously follow the advice given by the elders and the teachers who are serving Me by serving young children.

Shawnee has been suffering from false doctrine. She thinks that she should feel the Mystery and be Happy just because she is here. She thinks that she is supposed to be perfect just because she has a relationship to Me and because she gets up in the morning. But the older she gets, the more she realizes that this is not true—she cannot feel the Mystery or be

Happy or be perfect. She does not really understand this Way of life, and so she has developed a secret life.

Her secret is that she is not being Happy, she is not feeling the Mystery, and she is not perfect. She has not wanted to tell anyone that she has been being un-Happy, bereft of the feeling of the Mystery, and utterly imperfect, as if it is not known unless she says it. But I demanded that she say what her secret is, and since I did this, she became willing to say it.

Since she was not telling Me or anyone else any news, or anything we did not already know, when she confessed her secret, why do you think it was important that she say it? Because when she said it she became known and not hidden. She became real. Before that, she did not understand that her idea (that what was true of her was a secret from everyone) was an illusion, and that everyone could clearly see that she was un-Happy!

It is good that she understands this now. To make the confession of self-contraction, un-Happiness, and imperfection is the beginning of possibly being able to practice for real.

Shawnee is clearly expressing that she wants to be Happy, but she must understand that the only true Perfection is Happiness Itself, not anything she does or anything she looks like. Inherent Perfection is the Divine Reality, or Happiness Itself. If you want to be Happy, or really, Inherently Perfect, you must do what I ask you to do. Shawnee must do the practice I ask her to do—not because I ask her to do it, but because she understands it and therefore values it.

The way to be Happy, therefore, is to stop <u>doing</u> un-Happiness, and the way to stop doing un-Happiness is to do the opposite of un-Happiness.

Instead of putting attention on thinking, reacting, desiring, seeking, and fearing, Contemplate My bodily (human) Form, My Spiritual (and Always Blessing) Presence, and My Very (and Inherently Perfect) State, which is Happiness Itself. You will Realize Happiness if you do this. Contemplating the Realizer is Happiness Itself. I Call practitioners to practice devotional Contemplation of Me first and always, no matter what they are tending to think or feel or desire. Turn your attention 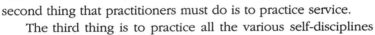 from whatever that is, and feel and Remember Me instead. The second thing that practitioners must do is to practice service.

The third thing is to practice all the various self-disciplines that I Give them. You cannot Contemplate Me unless you transcend your egoic self through service and self-discipline. You must submit your separate and separative self to Me through service and self-discipline. I Give people a great deal of self-discipline that covers every kind of contraction they might do.

If you practice those self-disciplines and serve Me and feel Me and Contemplate Me in every moment, then you will feel beyond the self-contraction in every moment, and you will be drawn out of your own contraction into My Very (and Inherently Perfect) State. If you do as I have just described, then you will be able to feel the Mystery and meditation will become real for you. Therefore, meditation is the fourth thing that practitioners must do.

Those who do this with great faith and feeling are purified relatively easily, and their Contemplation of Me becomes deep rather easily. People who really do this become exemplary devotees who are more and more purified of their qualities and increasingly Spiritualized. Eventually, they Realize That Which Is Perfect, That Which Is beyond all qualities.

People not so strong in devotion, service, self-discipline, and meditation have attention on their own self-contraction, so they do not grow so quickly, and practice does not become so deep so quickly. It is only when people become real and serious and constantly practice devotion, service, self-discipline, and meditation in relationship to Me that they truly begin to enjoy My Gifts and an increasingly Heart-Happy life. My devotees are Happy if they do what I tell them to do, which is to practice devotion, service, self-discipline, and meditation in relationship to Me. That is My Teaching Word to Shawnee and to all other children also.

You must talk to Shawnee about this. She must practice devotional Contemplation. She must feel beyond her separate and separative self by Contemplation of Me. She must study My Teaching Word for real and see how it applies to her life. Like Shawnee, all children must see how My Teaching Word applies to them, and they must practice service and all of the self-disciplines. They must feel beyond all thoughts and desires by Remembering Me. If Shawnee or anyone gets involved in thinking and reacting and desiring and seeking, he or she is immediately un-Happy. Therefore, in any moment, no matter what you are thinking, desiring, or fearing, Remember Me instead. In the same moment, apply whatever service and self-discipline applies in that moment.

Children must also understand and study the dietary discipline so that they understand the logic of it. And they must stop resisting self-discipline and acting as if they are stupidly deprived. They must live the proper diet that our doctors advise. In any case, stealing food is not a dietary matter. Basically, by taking food Shawnee is telling people that she is not practicing. She must be helped to practice the Way of the Heart.

Children, then, must practice devotion, service, self-discipline, and meditation in relation to Me and know why they must transcend themselves. They must discover Happiness by constant Remembrance of Me, and Realize Happiness Itself by feelingly Contemplating Me, and by doing all the self-disciplines I ask them to do.

This is not a silly, sugar-coated message. It is a real and true religious Communication. Shawnee and all children must be given the straight Wisdom-Teaching of the Way of the Heart, not some silly version of it concocted by those who resist it, and not a sugar-coated Sunday-school version that bypasses the realities that children know so well. Children, in their own fashion, must practice as seriously as any adult. To practice the Way of the Heart is just as difficult for them as for any adult. They ought to be able to communicate about these realities or difficulties, and also about the Happiness of their practice.

Likewise, children should constantly be served by the good company of teachers and parents who are exemplary in self-transcending devotion, service, self-discipline, and meditation.

Shawnee should have gotten a lesson from all of this, and she should understand and know what practice of the Way of the Heart is. Her guides must help her develop just this practice. Her practice of the Way of the Heart will not mature automatically. She will have to work very hard to go beyond her limitations.

If you approach Me rightly, you will receive My Spiritual Heart-Transmission, which will purify you and move you along in the process of the Way of the Heart. The more you practice, the more you will be purified of your limitations on your devotional response to Me, and the more deeply and more constantly you will feel My Divine Happiness in meditation and in daily life.

If Shawnee can understand this and accept My discipline of Happiness all the time, her living in the village will be a time to study and understand this lesson and discuss it with her guides. She must integrate My Wisdom-Teaching into her life as a real, true, and no longer secret practitioner.

Part of the discipline she must assume is to give up her criticism of others and her comparing herself with others. Her practice is her own responsibility, and, relative to this, she should not be concerned about the practice of others. She should simply make sure that her own practice is real. The way to make her own practice real is to give up all of her thoughts about others and her reactions to others, and to Contemplate Me with heart-felt devotion instead. When she has developed all of that, then she can again enjoy the privileges and practices of her membership in the Brahmacharya Order. How long it will take is up to her.

In the Village

by Sandra Kladnik

Heart-Master Da Love-Ananda said that Shawnee should come and live with me in the village and that we should share the same room. I already knew Shawnee a little, but we had never been intimate. When she arrived, I sensed her concern that I should like her and like living with her.

It was not long before she began to trust me. A breakthrough occurred when Kanya Remembrance came and talked with Shawnee some days after Shawnee moved to the village. During this conversation Kanya Remembrance

Sandra Kladnik, who has been a devotee of Heart-Master Da since 1973, shared her two-room cabin with Brahmacharini Shawnee for five weeks.

apparently told Shawnee that I had been a recluse at one time. Shawnee quizzed me about this and asked if I liked living with her. I said I liked it very much indeed. I also told her that Heart-Master Da had changed me, so that now I liked being with people. After that, I felt she was much more open with me.

I was struck by how naturally Shawnee presumed relationship in the village. She was not at war with her discipline, nor was she dramatizing any negativity. She did not hesitate to ask for what she needed, and she showed no signs of fear that what she asked for might be withheld. At the same time she accepted her surroundings as they were.

We talked about renunciation. She commented on the starkness of my room, which had no shelves, and asked me (for my own benefit) what I was going to do about it. I acknowledged that it was hard to have no shelves and that I hoped to have some eventually. But, I told her, if I did not get shelves, I would not get un-Happy about it. Shawnee seemed to agree that this was the best response.

Although Shawnee was not living the brahmacharya discipline, all the hours in her day were accounted for. Each morning, she did a routine of Surya Namaskar,[1] did her religious studies, and was tutored in academic

subjects. In the afternoons for about two hours she did kitchen service. Every evening I had dinner with her, which was an opportunity for her to talk about what had occurred that day and what she felt. She was under the specific discipline to confess her emotions and to communicate directly, rather than communicating indirectly through her behavior. She was also instructed to confront her tendency to fantasize and get in touch with reality. Heart-Master Da Love-Ananda was clearly Gifting Shawnee with an opportunity to grow up and express a new capability for practice through her stay in the village.

Shawnee wanted to know whether the discipline for the adults in the village was the same as that of the Brahmacharinis. I said that it was basically the same but that we were each responsible for self-generating our practice, as we were not observed as formally as the Brahmacharinis are. I told her, for example, that when I cooked for Heart-Master Da it was part of my job to taste the food I was preparing for Him. It was up to me to judge how much tasting was necessary and at what point it became an indulgence. Shawnee said that she would not like to be in the position of not being held directly accountable in her practice, and that she valued the help of being held to the discipline. When I heard her point of view about discipline and accountability, I saw my own limits more sharply.

I was deeply impressed by the purity of Shawnee's response to Heart-Master Da. There is no complication in it—she simply trusts Him completely. From time to time Shawnee saw Heart-Master Da Love-Ananda during her stay in the village. She was intoxicated by His Darshan and greatly helped by it each time she saw Him. Whenever I went to a Darshan occasion that she could not attend, she would wait for me to come back and ask me eagerly, "What happened? Did anything unusual occur?"

Over the five-week period that Shawnee lived with me, we both really opened up, lost face, and became very intimate. We expressed a great deal of love for each other. Apart from the fact that she was good company herself, her presence was a constant reminder to me of Heart-Master Da Love-Ananda. One day Shawnee was invited to attend formal Darshan for the first time since she came to the village. I was touched to see how happy she was about this. I wrote a passage in my diary as if I were writing to Heart-Master Da:

Your Love for Shawnee and Your Mastery of her breaks my heart. Seeing her turn to You, becoming intoxicated by Your Happiness at even a brief glance from You, seeing how Happy Your invitation to Darshan made her, her eagerness to have word of You in the form of stories about You—all are a wonderful testimony to Your transforming Spiritual Force. My heart opened tonight at Darshan when she came in with Kanya Remembrance to sit before You. I felt so much love for You tonight. Tears sprang from my eyes as soon as You entered The Giving Coat.[2] Your Love is Life, and it is our Joy.

The Giving Coat

CHAPTER TEN

What He Says
Is True

by Brahmacharini Shawnee

During my five-week stay in the village, I learned many things about my egoic tendencies and how to go beyond them.

The rooms I shared with Sandra were plain and bare with no shelves or furnishings except our beds. Due to the lack of shelving, I kept my clothes and other necessities on the floor covered by a towel in a small room at the back of our cabin. There was little decoration in the room, except for two pictures of Heart-Master Da Love-Ananda. This simple living circumstance was designed to leave my attention free for the process I was going through. All the usual tropical pests, including cockroaches, geckos, spiders, sandfleas, and mosquitoes, tried to share this simple space with me. They found their way in underneath the door, and in through the screens. Ants also seemed to love this room. They remade their homes inside my room daily, leaving tiny piles of dirt, wood, and other distasteful materials. A small spider lived in a crack right by my bed. Every night I would touch his legs with my pencil and force him back into his hole. I also tore his web nightly so he would discover I was not good spider company and go away. I accepted all of these trials as part of the ordeal and I was not un-Happy.

I did schoolwork, ate my meals, slept, and did all my practices in that room. I also served in the kitchen, cutting beans, Beans, BEANS! I cut green beans often, for the eighty people staying in the Ashram. I also did a number of other things, like peeling carrots, potatoes, onions, and garlic, helping to make breakfast for the Ashram and the lunch for Da Love-Ananda's weekly outing with the Brahmacharinis and the Kanyas.

As part of my discipline, I did not practice the brahmacharya disciplines—meditation, sacramental worship (or "puja"), formal occasions of seeing Heart-Master Da Love-Ananda (or "Darshan"), and listening to recitations of Heart-Master Da's Teaching Word. Most of all, I did not see my Heart-Master except when He walked to the library building near the kitchen, nor did I see the Kanyas or the Brahmacharinis. I could have nothing to do with animals, nor could I practice my sacred arts. I could not eat fruit or anything remotely like a sweet.

I did my academic studies, religious studies, Hatha Yoga, and conscious exercise. I served. The first few days seemed easy, because I was just settling in, and things were new and special. However, as time went on, I found out that this form of life was not at all exciting or "fun". I discovered that life in itself is a discipline.

I lived this way for many days, and then one night while I was studying in my room, I looked up through the window and saw Kanya Remembrance walking across the lawn. I stood up and watched her, thinking she was going across to the library or to see the teachers at the school. But she was coming toward my room! When she opened the door, I gave her a hug. We walked down to the beach, and I told her what I was feeling and what had been happening with me. From then on, every night when she could, Kanya Remembrance would come and talk to me.

Often we would walk down to the beach and talk about our relationship to Heart-Master Da Love-Ananda and the process He was bringing me through. One night, I asked her what an Enlightened person perceives. She suggested that I ask Da Love-Ananda, so I wrote this letter:

Dear Love-Ananda,[1]

I love and miss You and can't wait to see You again. I had a dream about You last night. Yesterday I served in the kitchen. We don't have our usual help on Sundays. I made salads and marinated vegetables, yams, potatoes, grated beets, and tomatoes for 80 people. I have been really missing You. I feel that there is something useful about not seeing You for this time. It makes me not take seeing You for granted so much because here I only see You when You walk to and from the library. So when I hear the conch[2] *I drop everything I am doing and run out to see You. Every second of Your Darshan is so precious. I watch You until I can't see even Your shadow.*

I can really appreciate Kanya Remembrance as a guide for me because she has gone through the same crisis I am going through. She helps me to make the commitment to real practice. I asked her last night when she came to talk to me about what I have been feeling—I asked her if You or any Enlightened person has a different perception of time, space, vision, sound, dreams, feelings, etc. She said to ask You. I think in a day or two I will be ready to take another step. I love You.

Love,
Shawnee

This is how He answered my question:

HEART-MASTER DA LOVE-ANANDA: Enlightenment has nothing directly to do with changing the perception of things. For example, if I look at a plant, it (generally) looks visually like a plant looks to everyone else. However, the Awakening to Divine Consciousness is a different Awareness altogether, a unique Awareness, of time and space, and of the Source of perception. Enlightened "perception" is that Awareness, rather than a different way of perceiving objects. There is a profoundly different Awareness of space and time and things, but not necessarily a different perception, although there could also (in some moments) be a different perception, depending on the characteristics of the

Enlightened person. The Enlightened person can be associated with siddhis [accomplishments, or powers], and therefore with a different perception. Such perception has nothing directly to do with Enlightenment Itself, however, but with how the Spiritual Energy is working through that person. So, potentially, as in My case, there can be occasionally (or as required) different perception and vision, but not necessarily.

When Kanya Remembrance came to my room, it was the first step toward my reintegrating with the other members of the Brahmacharya Order. After some time, I started to have my academic classes in the schoolroom again, and before too long I was attending class with the Brahmacharinis and was able to speak to them again.

Heart-Master Da Love-Ananda invited me to come and celebrate Kanya Suprithi's birthday with Him and the Kanyas and the Brahmacharinis. (I had presumed I would not be going because I had not been seeing Heart-Master Da Love-Ananda or having much contact with the Brahmacharinis.) On that day I was allowed to have fruit again and also some sweets, as it was a special occasion. It was wonderful to be with Heart-Master Da Love-Ananda and see Him Give Gifts to Kanya Suprithi.

After the birthday party, I went back to the village and continued my special discipline. Shortly afterwards, I was invited to go on an outing with Heart-Master Da Love-Ananda, the Kanyas, and the Brahmacharinis. I served the lunch, and so I was able to bring a serving disposition to my familiar intimate circumstance. On another occasion, the Celebration of the Raising of the Giving Tree,[3] I was invited to come to special meals with Da Love-Ananda and to decorate the tree.

These invitations to be in Heart-Master Da Love-Ananda's Company again were wonderful, but I was still experiencing difficulties in my practice. I would occasionally dramatize in school, or have an argument with one of the Brahmacharinis. In fact, just after the tree-decorating occasion, I dramatized by having an argument. I was given the consequence of not going on the outing with Heart-Master Da Love-Ananda that day. I was feeling very sad about this.

The next morning, as I was raking leaves and feeling that no one loved me because I am not perfect and because I had dramatized, I looked up and saw Love-Ananda walking slowly down the path from the library building. I sat down and bowed, expecting Him to walk right past me, to withdraw His Love from me because of my dramatization. So I was ready to withdraw my love. (I tend to think that when I dramatize, people will not love me, and so I withdraw my love first so as not to give them a chance to hurt me.) But I didn't have a chance to withdraw because all the while He was walking down the path He looked right at me. His Face was very loving and sweet. It was obvious He had not withdrawn His Love from me. As He came closer to me, He smiled and Gave me His Blessing by saying "Tcha".[4] I realized that I do not have to be perfect or look good or be a certain way for Heart-Master Da Love-Ananda to Love me. He always Loves everyone Perfectly.

That night Kanya Remembrance came to the village and told me that she was not going to come see me again until I stopped creating conflicts with the other girls. I had seen enough about myself, and now it was time to take responsibility! The next day, I practiced with great intensity and I did not get a single Da-Stick reminder in school. (A Da-Stick reminder is given when you violate some aspect of your discipline—such as to sit in a good asana,[5] or to respect your teacher, or to keep your environment clean, or to maintain positive speech, or to pay attention. If a violation occurs, the teacher takes a stick that is  kept in the various classrooms for this purpose and whacks it on the table quite loudly to remind you that you need to change your act!) I had been having trouble with this discipline because it was new and very strictly applied. You do not get the stick just for major dramatizations of "Narcissus". On one occasion the stick was given for there being one needle on a girl's desk. Perhaps she did not even see it, but since she did not keep her environment perfectly neat, she "got the stick". You could not get away with anything. That was hard for me, and I had gotten quite a few sticks until this day.

Heart-Master Da Love-Ananda also told me during this time that I am always "performing". I thought about this for a long time, as it was hard for me to understand what He meant. But the more I observed myself, the more I understood what He was saying—that I tend to try and look a certain way to get attention and love from others. I began to practice with this habit, and whenever I noticed that I was performing I would Remember Sat-Guru Da Love-Ananda instead and drop this unnecessary game.

I also noticed that on days when I Contemplate Heart-Master Da Love-Ananda and put more energy into my disciplines and practices, there is a change in my awareness. Usually I am just aware of what is happening in the moment, the narrow space of this time and place. But on the days when my attention is with Da Love-Ananda I notice my awareness expand. I perceive much more. I do not notice myself so much as an individual, separate being, but see myself from a different point of view. Instead of the ordinary feeling of "This is Shawnee doing this, this is Shawnee doing that," I feel much more expansive, more a part of everything. I feel clear, free, and Happy.

After this I was invited to the Kanyas' residence to take part in the weekly day of retreat with the Brahmacharinis and Kanya Remembrance. The next day Kanya Remembrance discussed with me whether it was time for me to be reintegrated with the other Brahmacharinis. That meant I would be doing all the brahmacharya disciplines, living with the Brahmacharinis, and seeing my Heart-Master, Da Love-Ananda. This was a very big step. We both felt it was time, so Kanya Remembrance wrote a letter to Da Love-Ananda to ask Him what He felt about it. He agreed.

I moved back into No Doubt Of God with the other Brahmacharinis. Originally, Kanya Remembrance thought that I would gradually reintegrate all

No Doubt Of God

the various aspects of brahmacharya life into my schedule over a period of days. But when He heard this plan, Heart-Master Da asked, "Why does it have to take so long?" So we changed our proposal and I took on all the disciplines in one day.

I have found that the discipline in the Brahmacharya Order is a very great demand. You must be committed to doing it because it is not at all easy. It requires great self-transcendence.

The brahmacharya discipline is much more intense than the discipline that I lived in the village, and so I had to adjust very quickly. Our schedule is very tight, and we do not have time to walk slowly, meander, get side-tracked, or go to other places than directly where we are supposed to be going. We have to be punctual. Our mealtimes are also very short. We do not have time to "space out" while we eat or lounge in a leisurely way after a meal. We maintain silence for the first five minutes of every meal, and we do not speak casually in a social manner at any time except during our scheduled intimate time. A lot of the time we observe silence. We are observed at all times. Someone walks with us when we move from place to place. We do not have the opportunity to get into arguments because there is someone there to stop them immediately.

And the Da Stick is another reminder. If you get three Da Sticks in one day, then you get the food discipline. The food discipline means that for a number of meals, maybe one, maybe five or even more, your diet consists of only the things that you really hate to eat. And everything is served cold. So a discipline diet might start out with cold oatmeal for breakfast, served with nothing but powdered soy milk or seed milk, both of which are really "horrible" drinks (they are nutritious, but we don't like the way they taste). For lunch, you might have cold rice with buckwheat sprouts (which are bitter), cold okra (which is slimy), "Fijian greens" (which are disgusting), possibly some seaweed or raw onions, and no dressing or sauces. For snacks during the day, you might have more powdered soy milk or seed milk. Dinner would probably be the same as lunch, perhaps with cold millet or buckwheat instead of rice.

Although this diet is nutritionally balanced, it is a very dreaded discipline, and you do everything you can to avoid it. Heart-Master Da is such a Genius in the way He Serves His devotees! He created the food discipline for children because it would reach us right where we live—in the food body! It helps us to really want to change.

All the Brahmacharinis learned very quickly. After the first day that I rejoined the others, nobody had the food discipline. Every night we went to see Heart-Master Da Love-Ananda, either just to say hello for five minutes or to spend a longer time with Him. Because I had not seen Love-Ananda regularly for some time, I was able to feel even more than before how wonderful it is to have the Grace of seeing Sat-Guru Da every single day, and being able to speak to Him, touch Him, and serve Him.

You may wonder why we practice these disciplines that are so difficult and demand self-transcendence when we could be doing whatever we want and eating whatever we want and living an egoic life. (I was caught wondering the same thing when I took the honey, but I soon found out!) The reason for our choice is that we trust and love our Sat-Guru, Da Love-Ananda. We know that what He says is true. We know it in our hearts. We know that we will not be Happy if we live the way the ego wants to live. We have tried this and it does not work. And so we give our lives to practicing and Realizing God. Heart-Master Da Love-Ananda has described our life as a "hard school" but a "Happy Way of life", and it really is.

Heart-Master Da Love-Ananda, 1990

Shiny and the "Bright"

Letters from Brahmacharini Shawnee

K ANYA REMEMBRANCE: Shawnee's time in the village was a very real and difficult ordeal for her, but through it she learned more and more to let go of the dark secret of being hidden and un-Happy and to accept and live in relationship to the "Bright" and Happy Secret of Who Da Love-Ananda Is and the Way of Happiness that He Reveals.

When we were living at The Mountain Of Attention just before she was initiated into the Brahmacharya Order, Heart-Master Da Love-Ananda Gave Shawnee the name "Shiny". She immediately loved it and understood that He had Given it to her to remind her to Shine beyond her tendency to be peculiar,[1] dark, and withdrawn. Since then, Shiny has used her new name often. As you can see in the following letters written to Da Love-Ananda while she was living in the village, the Gift of this ordeal in Shawnee's life was about truly becoming "Shiny"—bright with self-transcending practice.

Dear Love-Ananda,

I love You. I am typing You this letter tonight on the school typewriter. I hope You can read it (even though I'm still learning and making lots of mistakes!) Today I finished reading *The Love-Ananda Gita* and I started doing a writing assignment to help me to understand it. I also started reading *Water and Narcissus*.[2] I am finding my study really helping me understand my narcissistic tendencies. I really feel this time helping my practice. I hope You enjoyed the garnishes. I love making Your food because it keeps me always Remembering You and Your Great Love for all beings, and helps me to remember to do the same. I feel Happy (as if I just had a bath after not having one for a long time and washed away all my pent-up emotional excess so I can be true to my name, Shiny). I am working through the temptations of the self-contraction (definitely not perfectly yet, but I am working). Every day I feel my practice grow and I get more and more strong. I bow down in gratitude for Your Help and Guidance. Da!

Love,
Shiny

Dear Love-Ananda,

I love You. I fell into the sand trap today. I watched myself doing exactly what You were talking about. I mean <u>exactly</u>. The withdrawal, the secret-keeping, the self-contraction, the whole caboodle. Afterwards I saw each place where I should have done something different. I thought about what I was feeling, what I was trying to communicate in a childish way. I confessed my feelings to Sandra, and I told her all I felt and did, so that it wouldn't be a secret anymore. I see exactly where I should have practiced, what I should have said and done rather than do what I did. There is no one to blame but me. I created it. Next time I feel myself slipping into the trap I will know exactly what to do, and it will be just a choice of practice or dramatization. Very simple.

I chopped beans today. I was talking to Sandra about Contemplation of You. We talked about how we become what we meditate on. So if I meditate on You I become Happy like You. If I meditate on myself, on my un-Happiness and contraction, I become more and more like that. The previous one is the definite choice—but it takes work! It doesn't just happen. I miss You very much. I love You.

Love,

Shawnee (I don't deserve Shiny today)

P.S. Thank You for the Notes to remind me of my practice.

Dear Love-Ananda,

I love You. I re-read the Notes You Gave about me and my practice and tendencies. I again felt how useful they are to me. I feel how much my practice can grow if I fully make right use of them. Again, I feel so grateful to You and Your invaluable Instruction. Today I served in the kitchen. I enjoy that very much because it gives me an opportunity to put my energy into a creative and Happy service. Also, it keeps me connected to You because everyone there is doing everything as a direct service to You.

I love You.

Shiny

Dear Heart-Master Da Love-Ananda,

I love You very much. I have been feeling very open. My mind stops whenever I spontaneously Remember You and the things You sometimes say that are so completely unfathomable. I feel every second not spent in Contemplation of You is a precious second wasted. I must by Your infinite Grace Realize God in this lifetime. Who knows when I will have another chance like this? I feel on fire with inspiration. If ever I feel despair, that I am too weak and insignificant to receive the Grace of God-Realization, I remember Kanya Remembrance and Kanya Tripura and how they transcend themselves, and I take courage. I hope the words I have used are not jumbled and do not differ in meaning from what I am trying to express. I always have a hard time putting my feelings into words.

I love You.

Love,

Shiny

Dear Love-Ananda,

I love You. Every day I re-read the Notes You Gave me. I have under-lined the key points for me and it really inspires me. I have noticed that since I started living in the village, I have begun to view time in a differ-ent way. Every day is exactly the same and very simple, leaving more of my attention free to Contemplate You and know what I am supposed to be doing, moment to moment. I feel You so much when I work in the kitchen because I feel my relationship to You so strongly, knowing that You will eat this food, and it helps me put all my energy into making it with real energy and love. I am studying *Ashram Dharma* by Swami Muktananda.[3] I write down all the key points and consider them fully and how they fit into my circumstance. Also, I am going to start reading *Spiritual Cannibalism* by Swami Rudrananda.[4] I find many likenesses to the Way of the Heart in the Teaching of Swami Muktananda, but there are also differences. Thank You for this Way of life. I miss You a lot and know I will see You again when I clearly demonstrate my practice.

Love,
Shiny

Dear Love-Ananda,

I love You. I miss You very much. I have some stories on how in a given moment I chose to practice. (Of course there were a few times when I could have been more disciplined.)

I was working in the kitchen and I walked over to get a cup. Atelaite, who works in the kitchen, was cutting a watermelon. She offered me a piece. I told her I couldn't have fruit, even though I really wanted to eat it because watermelon is one of my favorite fruits. Another time, Elizabeth Dard-zinski asked me to fill several bowls with raisins and prunes. I had to dig my hands into them and not even eat one. It was a real test! I did not eat any.

Atelaite

Also, in the room I am staying in there are lots of geckos, ants, spiders, and cockroaches. I have to just ignore them. I haven't petted one cat since I got the "no animals" discipline.

Today I felt very tired. I had to keep putting out energy even though I felt lazy. At P.E. time I did a physical fitness test. I did 108 of everything except pushups. I did 27 of those. I have to work up to 108. I did 108 of the following: jumping rope, leglifts, jumping jacks, sit-ups, stair steps (the person must jump onto the stair with both feet touching it, then jump back down—this was the hardest part of the test), and running in place. I felt my energy coming alive. A little later I did some Surya Namaskars to help me "wake up".

Today in the kitchen I chopped beans. With each chop I would say the Name "Da" in my heart (and mind) and breath. This helped me keep my attention on You. I also sang devotional songs in my heart and mind because I can't sing them out loud. Every day I get distracted less and less. I demand more and more of myself.

There are two pictures of You here in my room. They are both so Happy that I start smiling and laughing every time I look at them. I feel like You are always watching me through these pictures (and everywhere else), so when I see them I remember that You are with me, and I smile at You. It was so wonderful to see You walking across the lawn today. You are so beautiful. It makes me Happy whenever I think of You. It was wonderful to see Kanya Remembrance and to talk to her again. When I was making garnishes in the kitchen, the cooks, Sandra and Paula, reminded me of the lesson they got about making garnishes too elaborate. (At The Mountain Of Attention they got carried away with making the fruit beautiful, and You reminded them that You only need a simple fruit dish.) I continued to do simple things like sorting seeds, cutting beans, etc., in alternation with special gifts for You, because it is truly all a gift. You don't care if it is a fantastic meal or just a simple flower if there is real devotion in it. Thank You for this time to rebalance and practice. I love You so much.

Love,
Shiny

Dear Sat-Guru Love-Ananda,

I love You. Thank You for inviting me to the Darshan occasion. It was so wonderful to see You again. I felt very happy to see You and be able to sing to You again. I am so grateful for this Gift of Darshan. I felt my love for You so strongly.

Today I was having math class. My teacher leaves the door open whenever he leaves. I have asked him if he would please remember to close it several times but he keeps forgetting. Today he left it open, and I lost my patience. I got up and closed the door noisily so he would remember. Then I realized I was communicating in a childish way. I reminded him again without being angry. He has started closing it more often now. It felt good to transcend myself like that.

Thank You again for inviting me to Darshan. I felt very Happy. I can't really describe it. I love You.

Love,
Shiny

Dear Love-Ananda,

I love You and miss You very much. Yesterday I served in the kitchen all day. I had a lot of time to simply Contemplate You. With each vegetable I chopped I worked out a certain rhythm, like for green beans. I cut off one end and say "Da", and then the other end and say "Da", then I cut it in thirds and say "Da", and then I put it in a bowl and take a deep breath.

The Fijians I work with are all very happy and they like their service in the kitchen. I thought about what You were doing while You were out at Long Beach today. Sandra told me all about how You Instructed everyone at the beach on how to long-jump!

I have been studying *Spiritual Cannibalism* and it is very useful to me because it is about being strong and very intense in practice. I also listened to an audio tape about Saint John of the Cross. I found a lot of the things he criticizes about beginning practitioners are exactly what I'm up to.

It was so wonderful to see You walking across the lawn yesterday! You are so majestic, so strong and powerful, so Happy! I am so grateful for Your Help. I love You.

Love,
Shiny

Dear Love-Ananda,

I love You. I was so Happy to hear that if I practice tomorrow I can come and see You and celebrate Kanya Suprithi's birthday. I had a much Happier day today than yesterday in that I practiced my disciplines and didn't create un-Happy circumstances. I am going to help make Kanya Suprithi's birthday cake tomorrow. I like making cakes even when I can't taste them, though I like it even better when I can taste them. I can't think of anything else now except seeing You again. I am so excited. I can hardly wait. I know the biggest test is going to be afterward. That is when it gets hard and I have to transcend myself.

When I work in the kitchen I always perk up my ears when I hear someone telling a Leela[5] of Your Divine Play or how You Test the practice of the cooks. I like to hear about how they respond, and how much attention they give to their service, so no seeds get in Your watermelon.

I love You.

Love,

Shiny

Dear Love-Ananda,

I love You. It was so wonderful to see You last night. You are so beautiful, equanimous, and graceful. I was so happy to see You, the Kanyas, and the Brahmacharinis. Today will be a big test of my practice after having all the special foods, etc. I am going to practice really hard. I loved seeing the beautiful jewelry that You designed. You are so creative and loving when You Give Gifts (all Gifts). I love You.

Love,

Shiny

Dear Love-Ananda,

I love You so much. I was so happy that You invited me to Darshan. During Darshan, I felt very calm and I felt like I was being pulled in and up at my ajna chakra.[6] I felt very relaxed.

I served in the kitchen yesterday. I peeled and sliced carrots in a big machine. I felt my love for You. I bow down in praise and gratitude for Your Teaching and Help. I love You.

Love,
Shiny

Dear Heart-Master Da Love-Ananda,

I love You with all my heart. I miss You so much. Today I served in the kitchen by cutting cabbage. I said "Da" with every slice. Every time I said it I felt Happier and Happier, for no "apparent" reason. I was just cutting cabbage, but today, because I was saying the Name, it made me feel Happy. I felt Happy just thinking of Your beautiful, radiant, smiling Face, and cutting cabbage. Usually when I say the Name I feel Happy and peaceful, but today I felt <u>really</u> Happy. It made me smile. When I Contemplate You, I picture You in my mind and heart, feel You, think about times I have seen You, and remember Leelas and stories about You (like the tapioca pudding story[7] and recent Leelas of Your Love and Blessing).

I have been practicing typing (so I can write easier) and have gotten up to an average speed of 40 words per minute. I can basically do the whole keyboard. I feel Happy every time I think of You. I prefer to talk about You above other things I used to talk about. It makes me smile, even laugh. When I look at these pictures of You here in my room, I smile. In one of the pictures, You have the most loving, soft, beautiful look that floods me with smiles of Happiness. In the other You have such a devilish look on Your Happy Face that I can't keep from laughing! They are both very Happy pictures. I feel completely distracted by You!

Love,
Shiny

Dear Love-Ananda,

I love You. I miss You so much. I talked with Kanya Remembrance last night. I told her that I really didn't want to be away from You. She told me I had to let myself feel that and not stuff it down. I told her that I have started to let myself think and feel things (especially doubt and fear) which I never used to let myself feel.

I have been studying an adult study course on *The Basket of Tolerance*.[8] I have found it very useful and demanding more of me. I have decided that I must devote my entire life to God-Realization if it's going to happen. I must practice intensely every second no matter what the circumstance. I must be fiercely devoted to living the discipline. I must shoot straight for the eighteenth hole. I have to generate my practice and "stop waiting for devotion to happen to me". I have to stop thinking "Oh, I have the whole rest of my life to Realize God, I can just indulge a little right now." No! I don't have all the time in the world. Who knows, I may die tomorrow. Then where would I be? I love You.

Love,
Shiny

Dear Love-Ananda,

I love You and miss You a lot. Today I transcended myself at two particular times (and more) that required a lot of me. The first time I was working at the Type Right, a small machine that teaches you how to type. I get really mad at it every time I work on it because I have to do the same exercise over and over and I have to punch the keys really hard to get them to register. It is like a torture machine for me. I just can't stand it. It makes me so mad, so frustrated. So today that happened and I was about ready to break the machine in little teeny pieces when I remembered my practice. I took a deep breath and dropped my anger and went to my next class Happily.

The second time I transcended myself was when I was working in the kitchen. The head cook asked me to chop onions. Onions make my eyes hurt really bad and give me a headache. Also, I had some splinters in my hand and I knew that it would sting. I <u>really</u> didn't want to chop onions. But I transcended myself and did anyway. I didn't have any of the expected reactions to the onions and even enjoyed chopping them.

I was watching the Kanyas a few times today as they walked across the lawn. I saw that no matter what they were doing, they were Remembering You. They are very exemplary and are obviously radiating Happiness no matter what they are doing. I saw how I wanted to be Happy and Remember You at all times no matter what, like them. I know how to do that and want to and will.

I love You,
Shiny

Dear Love-Ananda,

I love You. Thank You for inviting me on the outing and to dinner with You. I was so happy to see You. You are so Happy and beautiful. At the Arati[9] I felt full of joy. I closed my eyes and relaxed. I felt like I was drifting up out of my physical body. I also felt a knot right in my solar plexus. It was very definitely a knot. I also felt one in my heart and throat. I relaxed and tried to let them go by Contemplating You instead. They were pretty stubborn, but they did relax a little.

Yesterday, I feel, was a day when I kept my attention on You pretty much all the time. I am going to try and make all my days be like that. Every day I feel my practice growing. I learn new things. When I told Kanya Remembrance about how I liked things I had to really transcend myself in order to learn about, You said, "Tell her to try Spiritual life!" Now I am trying it and find it to be much better than any puzzle! Thank You for everything You have Given me so Graciously. I love You.

Love,
Shiny

Dear Love-Ananda,

I love You. I miss You very much. Today I finished my eighth grade math book. I am sending it to You if You want to look at it. I have continued reading *Spiritual Cannibalism*. Sometimes I think, "Why am I getting disciplined? Look at what the other girls are up to! etc., etc." But then I think, "It's good that I am dealt with so strongly, so that I have plenty of opportunities to transcend myself." I feel how lucky I am to be here with You. Then I am glad I am who I am and that I get dealt with as I do and I don't want to be someone else. I always remind myself, even though it is discipline and it is hard, that not doing it is even harder, and not truly Happy, but just deluding. I love You.

Love,
Shiny

Dear Sat-Guru Siddha,[10]

I love You. I worked hard on my academic studies today because I know that is one of my forms of Sat-Guru-Seva.[11] I have a picture of You by my desk and I look at it throughout my day. It reminds me to Contemplate You no matter what I am doing. I finished reading the autobiography of St. Therese of Lisieux. I admired her determination and one-pointedness. I also noticed where she made mistakes. She was making the fourth stage error—she thought God is a separate being and she had to do things as a separate person to please Him. I love You.

Love,
Shiny

Dear Sat-Guru Da,

I love You. Today I felt fluish so I had school in my room. I felt very dizzy and it was one of those days where I just didn't feel good. I feel better now. I practiced with my discomfort. I didn't become sluggish and weak. I put out energy in my studies and didn't dramatize a weak, peculiar attitude. I love you.

Love,
Shiny

Dear Love-Ananda,

I love You very much. Thank You for the Notes You Gave about my idealism and tendency to "perform". I can feel how they are true. I am grateful for all of the Help and Instruction You have Given me. I love You.

Love,
Shawnee

Dear Love-Ananda Da,

I love You very much. Today I didn't get one Da-Stick reminder. I practiced hard to remember my disciplines and asana. It felt much Happier than dramatizing. I felt balanced. I finished my spelling workbook and I am sending it over with this letter. My spelling is improving greatly but it is still one of my weak points. I spell "through" like "threw", for example.

I am working a lot on gifting projects now in preparation for The Feast of God in Every Body.[12] I hope I have not been idealistic in this letter. I love You.

Love,
Shiny

Dear Love-Ananda Da,

I love You so much. It was so wonderful to see You yesterday. I hope You enjoyed the day and don't feel wiped out. It was a perfect way to begin God in Every Body Day.

Thank You for this wonderful day. I love You.

Love,
Shiny

Dear Love-Ananda Guru,

I love You so much. It was so wonderful to be able to see You two times today. At the Darshan occasion I felt my love for You so strongly I could hardly sing. I felt very Happy to be there. In the place where my ribs meet, I felt something that was like a fire. It started there and surrounded me in its flames. Several times a flame would extend up my throat and it would make me yawn.

When You came home from The Matrix[13] and drove past, You smiled at me and waved. It made me very Happy.

Heart-Master Da Love-Ananda at The Feast of God In Every Body, 1988

While You were gone today, I practiced blowing the conch in the walk-in refrigerator (so no one would think You were coming), so I can blow it when You come into the village. I served in the kitchen all day. I helped make the picnic lunch. Kanya Remembrance told me about how You pretended You were being eaten by a shark and she almost believed You! It made me laugh.

This morning I woke up at 4:20. A bug was buzzing around in my ear. It couldn't get out. It was flapping its wings. I could feel its little feet fluttering around. I started to get scared because it would not come out. Then I started breathing and relaxing. The bug calmed down and Laurel Patterson came and gave me some Q-tips. Eventually I got it out. Transcending fear is different from transcending anger. I love You and miss You a lot.

Love,
Shiny

Dear Love-Ananda Hridayam,

I love You. Today I dramatized in school. I feel bad about it after going to the occasion yesterday. I feel like I have to try and make it up somehow. I know that I must consistently practice the discipline and stop being a disturbance. I am eating a discipline diet for five meals as a consequence for my behavior. I know I deserve it. I love You.

Love,
Shawnee

Dear Love-Ananda Hridayam,

I love and miss You very much. Yesterday I fell in the sand pit again. I wanted to do what I wanted to do. After a while, I remembered what You told me and I started to talk about what I was feeling, doing, etc. Nonetheless, it happened and I will have to try again. It doesn't matter why it happened, it was really my responsibility to practice and I didn't. (Total imperfection.) I knew it was going to be "one of those days".

Yesterday, for the first time I was allowed to cut Your watermelon. It is actually harder than it looks. It took me about six watermelons to get it right. I started to write about "the honey incident" for the book yesterday. I love You.

Love,
Shawnee

Dear Love-Ananda Da,

I love You so much. I miss You. I have been living in the village for a month now. That is the longest time I have ever been away from You.

In science class we have been learning about cells, tissues, muscles, bones, organs, and reception-release.[14] We learn lots of big names for things and how they work together. There are so many names I'm starting to wonder if there is a name for each of the 100 million cells.

I have been doing grounds work. I rake a lot of leaves and pick up breadfruit leaves (as a result I think my arms are getting stronger). I also made two incense circles at the school with sand in them. I swept all the porches twice.

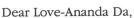

I love You,
Love,
Shiny

Dear Love-Ananda Da,

I love You. I miss You very much. I didn't get any Da Sticks today. In science class we studied about what sand is made of. We went down to the beach and found some of the elements that make up sand. We used a magnet and a lot of little tiny black pieces stuck to it so we knew it was magnetite. In English class we are all doing reports. We research things and learn how to write a report. I am writing one on polar bears. We are learning to find our own spelling mistakes. In history I am doing a report on the shaman or American Indian medicine man. I also did a lot of God in Every Body Day preparation—but I can't tell You about that. I love You.

Love,
Shiny

Dear Love-Ananda,

I love You so much. I miss You. It was wonderful to have a retreat and see You going to and from The Giving Coat. We worked on *The Two Secrets (yours, and Mine)*, and did gifting and study. The title You have Given for the book is so wonderful. Thank You. I love You.

Love,
Shiny

Walking to The Giving Coat

"Am I Feeling the Mystery Right Now?"

by Brahmacharini Shawnee

I had been living with the other Brahmacharinis in No Doubt Of God for about a week. Then one night after we had said goodnight to Heart-Master Da Love-Ananda, Kanya Remembrance and I were lying on her bed talking. I asked her about her practice, and I also asked her what her meditation is like. She asked me, "Can you feel that you are not just the body or the mind? When you are asleep or dreaming, you are not presuming that you are the body, are you? So can you feel that you are more than the body? You are more than what you look like. You witness, or watch, everything. You seem to be this hunk of flesh and blood, but don't you feel you are more than that? Stretch out your leg in front of you and look at your foot. Is that foot you? Wiggle it. You are apparently controlling the wiggle, but are you down there in your foot? Now look at a door across the room. Are you any more your foot than you are the door?

You are the awareness that is aware of the foot of this body you are animating. But is the body You? . . . No!"

She was telling me in her own words what Heart-Master Da Love-Ananda Reveals to everyone. This is how He says it in *What and Where and Who To Remember To Be Happy:*

<u>You</u> aren't anything you know or feel or see or hear or look like or name or think. All these things just happen, and <u>you</u> get to watch or know or think them. <u>You</u> feel and see your own body or your inside sounds or lights or dreams or all the places that come up.

You think the names of *and* *and* *and* *and* *and*

You even think "I" and "me" and "mine". Well, what are you if you only watch all of these things?

You are the Mystery! Yes. And you don't know what <u>you</u> <u>Are</u> either! Yes. There <u>Is</u> <u>Only</u> the Mystery! And you yourself in your Heart and up and down and in and out <u>Are</u> the Mystery. It <u>Is</u> All One Feeling.

If you will remember every day to feel and breathe the Mystery, and if you will remember to feel that you are more than what you look like, and if you will remember to Be the Mystery Itself, then you will be happy every day. And all kinds of more than wonderful happenings will come up for you. You will feel happy and you will always help and love others, even those who are having

---

trouble feeling happy and are even trying to make you forget the Mystery.

It is good to spend a lot of your time talking about the Mystery with others, instead of talking about unhappiness and things that happen when you forget to love. People who also feel the Mystery and love It are the best friends to have, because they always remind you to feel the Mystery and to be happy and to love.

I have always been remembering and feeling and breathing and loving and Being the Mystery. And I was born so that I could be everyone's Friend, by Showing them the Mystery, and Teaching them about the Mystery, and Helping them to remember and feel and breathe and love and Be the Mystery.

I am Heart-Master Da Love-Ananda. And I will always forever be remembering and feeling and breathing and loving and Being the Mystery.

And all My friends can easily always forever remember and feel and breathe and love and Be the Mystery, if only they remember Me, and feel Me, and breathe Me, and love Me, and so forget themselves, and forget their unhappiness, and forget even what they look like, and remember only Me.

And those who truly and completely remember only Me find it easy to remember to Be the Mystery, because I Am the Mystery Itself, here and "Bright" for all.[1]

Kanya Remembrance told me, "That awareness is a feeling. Can you feel that feeling-awareness? That feeling-awareness is What you Are. Heart-Master Da Love-Ananda calls this feeling-awareness 'Consciousness' or 'the Mystery'. It is the Feeling of Being What you really Are rather than the feeling of seeming to be what you look like."

Then I asked her, "What does it feel like to feel the Mystery?"

She answered me, "Well, even though the Mystery or Consciousness is one Feeling, which is the Feeling of Love-Ananda, everybody may feel or describe it differently, depending on their stage of practice."

So I asked my real question, "How would I feel it?"

Kanya Remembrance told me, "When you Contemplate Heart-Master Da Love-Ananda, you can see Him and hear Him with your feeling. If you picture or see Heart-Master Da Love-Ananda either in your mind or in a photograph, you also feel What He Feels like or What He Is. You don't just see Him or hear Him or look at Him, but you feel Him."

As she talked, I did as she said. "Can you feel Him?" she asked. I told her I could feel Him. She asked, "Does that feel Happy?" and I answered, "Yes, it does." She asked me where I felt the feeling of Heart-Master Da, and I told her I felt it in my heart. She said, "Yes."

I said, "It feels Happy. It feels warm. It feels tingly. Does this mean that I am feeling the Mystery right now?" When she said "Yes," I was quite surprised and very Happy because I saw that I could feel the Mystery.

Then I told Kanya Remembrance that when I was eight years old, Heart-Master Da Love-Ananda had Blessed me at the Love of the God-Man Celebration.[2] I had felt the Mystery very strong. But then I began to think that that was the way I was supposed to feel the Mystery all the time. I thought that the feeling of the Mystery had to be extremely strong or it was not real. But Kanya Remembrance told me, "No, it does not have to be like fireworks. It is just a simple Happy and Free feeling. Sometimes you might feel warm and tingly, and sometimes you might feel other effects of the Mystery, or sometimes the body-mind might not feel good at all, but you can always feel the Mystery! That is feeling Heart-Master Da Love-Ananda, the feeling of Who your Heart-Master really Is."

This made me very Happy, because I realized that I could feel the Mystery, and I was feeling it right then. I could see even more clearly that what Heart-Master Da Love-Ananda has told me about how to practice Happiness is true because now I could feel the Happiness of the Mystery! Even though I had felt this feeling before, it had not been very strong, so I did not think it was the Mystery. But now I saw that when I practiced Contemplation of Heart-Master Da, I felt the Mystery stronger, so strong that I no longer had to doubt that I could feel the Mystery. I saw that the un-Happy self-contraction is purified by His Grace when I give Him my feeling and attention by living the disciplines and serving. I could understand how the practice works! I was very excited about this, and very grateful because I knew that it was only by Heart-Master Da Love-Ananda's Grace that this feeling of the Mystery becomes obvious to me.

This is how I practice feeling the Mystery: I picture Heart-Master Da Love-Ananda in my mind, or I look at a photograph of Him, or I remember times when I have been with Him. I let my heart open to the feeling of Him. When I do this, I feel a Happy feeling in my heart. It feels very peaceful, simple, and Happy. I feel joyful. And I feel like my eyes are shining with that Mysterious, Happy feeling.

**Heart-Master Da Love-Ananda
at the Love of the God-Man Celebration, March 4, 1984**

The day after my conversation with Kanya Remembrance I kept Contemplating Heart-Master Da Love-Ananda and I felt the Mystery and I was very Happy all day. I did not even get any Da-Stick reminders! That night Kanya Remembrance and I talked about my taking on full participation in the Brahmacharya Order again. I had already taken on my earlier privileges and responsibilities, but I was still not formally acknowledged as a fully active member of the Brahmacharya Order. We both felt that it was now time. When Kanya Remembrance later asked Heart-Master Da Love-Ananda if I could return to the full discipline of the Brahmacharya Order, He Gave His permission and said that we should decide on a good time. So, on the 15th of January, 1989, I participated in a ceremony of re-affirmation of my Brahmacharya vow and practices. I am glad that I went through this ordeal, and I am grateful to Love-Ananda for His Help. I can truthfully say that I feel that my practice is strong now, and that I do feel the Mystery and I know how to practice feeling that feeling.

Here is part of the prayer that Kanya Remembrance and I offered at the ceremony to Heart-Master Da Love-Ananda in gratitude for His Blessing and Instruction. Kanya Remembrance speaks first:

Beloved Heart-Master Da Love-Ananda,

We are extremely grateful for Your Blessing and constant Guidance of Your Brahmacharinis, Shawnee, Io, Tamarind, and Naamleela. Your Gift of the Brahmacharya Order in May 1988 has made profound and auspicious changes in the lives of these girls. You also Blessed Brahmacharini Shawnee with the Calling to meet the discipline of Your Brahmacharya Order without confusion, resistance, or misunderstanding. It is a Gift that she has been Given this opportunity to demonstrate her clarity, understanding, and commitment. Your Instruction, Guidance, and Blessing have awakened her to a steady depth of commitment and responsiveness that enables her to practice the brahmacharya discipline of the Way of the Heart for real. She has naturally and responsibly shown that she can now practice by using all of the Gifts of discipline You Give in this Sacred Way. She accepts Your Guidance and Help. She practices Contemplation, service, and self-discipline. She acknowledges, understands, and receives Your Seven Great Gifts.[3]

It is now time for her to show the visible sign of her Brahmacharya vow and practice by wearing again the sacred shawl You Gave her at the time of her initiation into the Brahmacharya Order. This shawl is the sign of her concentration in You, and adherence and submission to Your Mastery. May she also be Blessed to wear her mala again.

You have Blessed all the Brahmacharinis with the life-giving and heart-felt sign of the color green. Brahmacharinis Shawnee, Io, Tamarind, and Naamleela will now honor this Gift by wearing green uniforms.

Brahmacharini Shawnee and all the Brahmacharinis have studied their vows and they understand their disciplines. They gratefully acknowledge the great Instruction and Help to grow in their brahmacharya practices that You have Given them since their initiation in May 1988.

The Upanayana Initiation is real. Your Blessings are Active in the lives of Your Brahmacharinis. They are truly Yours to Master. They are Happy this is so. Their responsive self-understanding and submission to You, Sat-Guru Da, Who are the Divine Person Incarnate, is their Happiness.

May Brahmacharini Shawnee honor these Gifts forever.

Om Sri Da Love-Ananda Hridayam

Sat-Guru Da Love-Ananda Hridayam,

I love You very much. I thank You for this time of discipline. It has helped my practice a lot. I now know very clearly what my practice is. I will practice this devotion, service, self-discipline, and meditation. I bow down in gratitude at Your Feet.

Da

Shawnee Brahmacharini

"Get your Strength by Resorting to Me"

by Brahmacharini Io

One day while Shawnee was still living in the village, Tamarind Brahmacharini, Naamleela Brahmacharini, and I, because we had been particularly unwilling to practice that day, got the food discipline. When we went over to see Da Love-Ananda that evening, He said, "What is this I hear about the girls getting the food discipline?" I began to feel very small and did not want to look at Him. Kanya Remembrance said that we had been given the food discipline because we had been unwilling to practice in school. Heart-Master Da Love-Ananda began to talk to her in a very stern tone, saying, "Why do you allow them to get away with this? Wasn't there someone watching them? Why did they let them off the hook?"

Kanya Remembrance tried to answer as best she could. I started to see that I was the one who had not been practicing. No one else was responsible. I got very angry with myself for being so stupid, and I had the large lump in my throat that I get when I feel any emotion that I do not like.

Kanya Remembrance told Love-Ananda that she would never let this happen again, and that if it did happen again, she thought our discipline should be magnified. Heart-Master Da was silent for a moment and then He said, "Well, you tell me if it does happen again, and their discipline will be magnified!"

We said goodnight and left the room. Brahmacharini Tamarind and I silently ate our horrible discipline meal and cleared our dishes and went with Lynne to the school for homework.

On the way we began to tell Lynne about what had happened at dinner.

"Well, girls," she said, "If I were you, I would really start shaping up! You never know what might happen. You might even end up in the village like Shawnee. It is bad enough having her gone! If all of you were there, it would be horrible! Horrible!"

I felt really bad and I knew that somehow I had to make a change. We had religious studies that night, and so we kept on talking with Lynne about what we were feeling. Brahmacharini Tamarind and

In the classroom with Lynne

I were both very emotional. Lynne asked us if we had anything to confess, like Shawnee had. "Well," I said, "I have some trouble meditating but definitely not as bad as Shawnee. But I hate school. It is really hard for me."

Lynne asked me if I felt I really could practice, and I said, "I can't say. I don't think I have enough will to do it." I was extremely frustrated with myself and also very emotional. I cried while I confessed all this, but after a while I started to feel very relieved at having made this confession.

The next day was our day to spend time with Heart-Master Da Love-Ananda and the Kanyas. We served all morning as we usually do, and then Da Love-Ananda called us to go on an outing with Him. While we were waiting, Kanya Remembrance came into the room and said, "Well, Io Brahmacharini, Heart-Master Da has Given some very wonderful Instructions for you," and she called us to come over to the table. "This is what He said."

HEART-MASTER DA LOVE-ANANDA: The confession that you and Shawnee are both making is a confession of the ordinary part of you. You should start using the part of you that is Me to help you practice.

You get your tendencies not only from your parents but also from your past births (or your total history previous to being in this body). You are made up of many different qualities, those of your present parents as well as your own tendencies that are based upon your history previous to this birth. It is from Me, as your Sat-Guru, that you get strength and capability for self-transcending practice and for receiving My Seven Gifts associated with Realization.

When you are making a complaint in your characteristic way, what you are doing is identifying with your tendencies. The qualities and characteristics that you confess are just qualities of Nature that are not really true of you. You have a relationship to Me as Sat-Guru. You have the capacity to transcend those tendencies through receiving My Gifts and through practicing. You get your strength by resorting to Me.

Either you get your strength by resorting to Me or you end up with your ordinary traits and destiny. You do not, of yourself, have the capability to Realize the Divine. You must resort to Me as Sat-Guru, and you must do sadhana and receive My Gifts.

The tendencies that you inherit are ordinary, and so you are always going to say that you are not strong enough to practice and that you cannot do it. But your tendencies are not actually true of you. Everybody has different tendencies, but in fact they are not different—they are all made of the same stuff. They are made of positive, negative, and neutral. It is just electronics. Because everyone has all these tendencies, everyone has to practice by resorting to the Sat-Guru and His Gifts. You must grow up and accept responsibility, and transcend your egoic self, rather than indulge your egoic self. You must grow up and be human.

If you do not do this, things will get weirder and darker and more painful. But if you do it, things will get clearer, and you will move more and more into the Divine, or the Samadhi of the "Bright" Divine Condition.

You, Io, tend to be lazy, and so everyone around you will be demanding that you not be lazy. We will be constantly addressing your laziness and telling you that you must transcend this automatic tendency. People will serve you in this manner. And by confronting and meeting this real demand, you will be initiated into the third stage of life.

It is now time for you older girls to enter into the third stage of life. It is a moment like the bas mitzvah[1] that traditionally occurs at your age, the age of thirteen. It is time for you to accept real self-discipline and to change now. If you do not, your life will become very complicated and disturbed.

The expectation relative to children who are brahmacharis living in an Ashram is different than the expectation that is applied to other children, because brahmacharis who live in an Ashram have a much greater opportunity. Children who live in the usual social world go to the world. Brahmacharis who live in Ashram also live in the world of relations and things, but they practice the Way of God-Realization. You must realize, Io, that you do not have any choice. You must realize that life is not going to let you off the hook. Life does not let people off the hook. If you give life a stick, it is going to beat you over the head with it. If you do not practice and do the sadhana, you are going to get beaten over the head by life itself. That is the Law.

Therefore, you must practice, and everyone here is going to help you to be able to do it. One way everyone here is going to help you is to tell you that you are full of baloney. So, when you say that you cannot practice, no one here is going to believe it, because it is not true. In other words, you are just going to have to do it. You are going to be obliged to do it. Your tendency to feel you cannot do it is not true. It is just a characteristic of Nature that you must not identify with, because it is not you. Use your relationship to Me. Resort to Me, and practice the Way of the Heart as I have described it.

While we were still hearing these Notes, Heart-Master Da came in and asked if we had heard everything He had said yet. We told Him we had a little more to cover. Kanya Tripura offered to show Him a few things while He waited, so He went into the back room with her. When Kanya Remembrance had finished communicating all of His Instructions to me, she asked me if I had any questions and how I felt. I did not have any questions, but I felt very Happy and grateful for Love-Ananda's Instructions.

Just then, Heart-Master Da came in wearing a fantastic hat made from a big gourd. We all laughed. He pretended to be very serious and asked us, "What are you all laughing about?" Then He smiled and we started our walk to Turtle Cove. On the way, Heart-Master Da started talking about His gourd hat. He talked about giving retreatants and Ashram residents different kinds of hats, all made out of melons. Then He said, "We could give Io a bread hat when she just feels like loafing around. And we could give Shawnee a bucket-full-of-water hat to wear when she just wants to go with the flow." Everyone started laughing.

When we arrived at the picnic site, Heart-Master Da Love-Ananda told us we could go swimming before lunch. We swam around for a while and then came back to the beach to sit with Him. I am trying to break a bad habit of biting my nails. While we were sitting on the beach, I unconsciously started biting them. Da Love-Ananda caught me at it and began to explain to me why it is that I bite my nails. He said, "The reason you bite your nails is because your fingers and arms are always out in the world, and when you are anxious about something, you want to pull them in, and so you bite your nails. Nails are just body parts that grow back. If you did not have nails, you would end up biting right down to your elbow!"

We all laughed and were amazed at Heart-Master Da Love-Ananda's ingenious way of figuring things out. I am very grateful for His Help with my practice and how humorously He deals with my un-Happy tendencies.

Heart-Master Da Love-Ananda in His gourd hat

THE SEQUEL

$\bullet$ $\bullet$ $\bullet$

ONE
YEAR
LATER

"Green Is Here"

by Kanya Remembrance

The sacred emblem of The Hridaya Da Gurukula Brahmacharini Mandala

Since the Brahmacharinis' initiation into the Brahmacharya Order, they have been Graced with Heart-Master Da's Wise Instruction, Helping them to understand the real meaning of that initiation. They have been through an ordeal of testing and have passed the test by demonstrating their commitment to brahmacharya practice and making many dramatic changes in response to their Brahmacharya Heart-Master, Da Love-Ananda. Their love for Him and commitment to Him has been very obvious.

Because the Brahmacharinis made good use of the Gifts of practice that He had Given them, Heart-Master Da Love-Ananda Offered them even greater Gifts of practice in a formal ceremony of re-affirmation one year after their Upanayana initiation. This is when He Gave the Brahmacharini Order its formal name—The Hridaya Da Gurukula Brahmacharini Mandala. He has also made it clear that, although many

The Hridaya Da Gurukula Brahmacharini Mandala

young people may choose brahmacharya practice in the Way of the Heart (and all such brahmacharis are given over to Him and are intimate with Him by virtue of their practice), The Hridaya Da Gurukula Brahmacharini Mandala will always be a unique and distinct Mandala within our culture.

The Brahmacharinis, like the Kanyadanas, are unique in that they are Blessed to receive Heart-Master Da Love-Ananda's Personal and daily Instruction and Guidance. Because of their unique relationship to Him, Heart-Master Da also Gave a most auspicious Gift—Stating that they would now all be known by a name most directly associated with Him, the name "Free Jones". Now they are Brahmacharini Shawnee Free Jones, Brahmacharini Io Free Jones, Brahmacharini Tamarind Free Jones, and Brahmacharini Naamleela Free Jones.

Heart-Master Da Love-Ananda has also Blessed the Brahmacharinis with the Gift of wearing the tilak. Women in India have worn the tilak (a dot of red kum-kum powder worn in the middle of the forehead) for many centuries. The tilak was originally worn as a sign of loyal Remembrance or steadfast devotion to God. Heart-Master Da Love-Ananda has told us that, in the Way of the Heart, the basic message of the tilak is, "Forget self by Remembering the Sat-Guru." By wearing the tilak all the time (as the Kanyas also do), the Brahmacharinis are reminded not to forget the self and then Remember Sat-Guru Da, but to forget the self by Remembering Sat-Guru Da.

The practice of using kum-kum is not exclusive to the Kanyas and the Brahmacharinis—all devotees in the Way of the Heart place a little ash and kum-kum on their foreheads when they enter a Communion Hall for devotional practice. The ash signifies that devotees renounce or let go of their un-Happiness and their self-centeredness, just like throwing it away in the sacred fire. The kum-kum dot is placed on top of the ash to indicate that the way to throw away un-Happiness is by constantly Remembering Sat-Guru Da or constantly feeling-Contemplating Sat-Guru Da's bodily (human) Form, His Spiritual (and Always Blessing) Presence, and His Very (and Inherently Perfect) State. Because the Kanyas and the Brahmacharinis are formal renunciates and because of their unique relationship to Heart-Master Da, they wear this sign perpetually as a service to all others.

Earlier in the year, Heart-Master Da Love-Ananda had Blessed the Brahmacharinis with the Gift of wearing the life-giving color green (which is associated with the heart in our Way) for use in their formal uniforms. Now He Gave them the Gift of the traditional sari as their new uniform. From now on they would wear saris at school and at all sacred occasions.

This formality serves their practice of Remembrance of Heart-Master Da. These, then, are the signs of The Hridaya Da Gurukula Brahmacharini Mandala: the formal name for the Mandala, the name "Free Jones", the saris, the color green, and also the tilak.

In this ceremony of re-affirmation, the Brahmacharinis accepted, read aloud, and formally signed a sacred brahmacharya vow that outlines the Spiritual laws alive in their relationship to Heart-Master Da Love-Ananda. They had been tested for a full year since their initiation into the Brahmacharya Order and now their vow, which was developed during that year, spelled out all the agreements, disciplines, and forms of practice in the Way of the Heart that they had committed themselves to as members of The Hridaya Da Gurukula Brahmacharini Mandala.

When Heart-Master Da Love-Ananda saw that their vow was full and complete, He Blessed it with His approval and called us to perform the ceremony of re-affirmation. By Giving the Brahmacharinis these wonderful Gifts in this ceremony, Heart-Master Da Love-Ananda acknowledged the Brahmacharinis' clearly demonstrated commitment to practicing the brahmacharya Way that He Offers. (And He further Blessed the Brahmacharinis by Instructing us to perform this ceremony once each year on the anniversary of their Upanayana initiation.)

Now, in the second part of *The Two Secrets (yours, and Mine)*, the Brahmacharinis will tell the story of their re-initiation and some of the useful (and even humorous) lessons they have learned.

CHAPTER FIFTEEN

It Rained a Lot

by Brahmacharini Shawnee

T omorrow was to be a most auspicious day.

Tonight was May 4, 1989—the night before our re-initiation. We were all excited, but also serious, feeling what tomorrow would be like and what it would mean for our practice. After saying goodnight to Sri Da Love-Ananda, all the Brahmacharinis gathered in a circle at Owl Sandwiches, the Kanyas' residence at The Matrix, to prepare for the ceremony. We began our meeting with a prayer—the children's Invocation. Then Kanya Remembrance opened a thick folder of Instructions from Heart-Master Da Love-Ananda. She told us that tomorrow Sri Gurudev would be Giving us many Gifts. We would be receiving a formal name for our Brahmacharya Order—The Hridaya Da Gurukula Brahmacharini Mandala. He was also, for the first time, Giving all of us the Spiritual name "Free Jones", a name most wonderful to us because it is based on His own Names. We would begin wearing the tilak, and we would also begin wearing green saris as our new brahmacharya uniform.

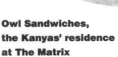

Owl Sandwiches, the Kanyas' residence at The Matrix

I felt very grateful for these Gifts. I knew that they were a sign that it was time to take on even greater responsibility for my practice. I thought back on the last year and on how much Happier I had become and how I had grown in my practice. I knew that I had not done anything but simply trust Heart-Master Da and do what He told me to do. It had all occurred by His Grace. I went to bed anticipating the Mysterious and sacred events of the next day.

At the beginning of the initiation the next morning, we offered a Statement of Intention, thanking Heart-Master Da Love-Ananda for all He has Given us. Then we all walked into the ocean to purify and wash away all our un-Happy tendencies. It was 9:00 A.M. The initiation had begun.

We submerged ourselves in the water, releasing our un-Happiness and self-concern. The Kanyas wore white saris, and we (the Brahmacharinis) wore green uniforms, not our saris yet. We offered a gift into the ocean, and then we went completely under water. After that, we walked to Baptized Each One, which is a large tree that Sri Gurudev has Blessed. (Now, it radiates the Feeling of the Mystery to all who come there.) We offered more gifts into a small sacred fire nearby.

As part of the initiation ceremony, Kanya Tripura read a description of the Gifts Sri Gurudev was Giving us and what they meant for our practice. The whole time I listened to the readings, I thought about what these Gifts would mean in terms of changes I must make now. But mostly I Contemplated Sri Gurudev and felt very happy about the wonderful Gifts He was Giving to us on this day.

Then, as part of the ceremony, we received our green saris. After we had changed into them, we went into Owl Sandwiches and sat in meditation for a time. After a while, Heart-Master Da walked in and took His Seat in front of us. He looked very intense, but very Loving and very pleased.

We each approached Heart-Master Da where He Sat, so Still and Full of Happiness. Each of the Brahmacharinis bowed and offered Him a small gift. He Anointed each of us in turn, Placing His thumb in red kum-kum and then Pressing His thumb into the middle of our foreheads. He looked at each of us the entire time we were in front of Him. All four of the tilak dots were perfect and full with His thumb print. When I went up to Him, He looked directly into my eyes as He gently but firmly placed the tilak on my forehead.

I felt how much I must strengthen my practice, use these Gifts, and relinquish all my un-Happy tendencies. I felt His Love so profoundly, and it was made even more clear how fortunate I was to be born into this circumstance—where it is understood that God-Realization is the only reason for being alive.

Then we filed out of Owl Sandwiches and went back to Baptized Each One. We sat by the great tree on the edge of the ocean and read our vows out loud, still feeling Heart-Master Da's Divine Grace. While we were reading, it began to rain. It rained really hard for quite a while, but we just kept on reading the vows. We got quite soaked, but it was a warm rain and no one minded at all because we felt so full of the Mysterious Feeling of Happiness that Heart-Master Da Love-Ananda Gives and Is. Then we went back up to Owl Sandwiches and signed our vows.

Later that night Sri Gurudev looked them over and He noticed that we had all printed our "signature". We had not written in cursive. He called us back to re-sign them in front of Him. He watched us as we signed them, this time in cursive. I felt that I was making a direct vow to Him even more, because now He had watched us actually sign the vow. He also asked us if it had rained while we were reading the vows, and we said, "Yes." He asked, "Just a little or a lot?" And we said, "A lot." And He said, "Good!" And we understood that the rain was a Blessing.

After we had all signed our vows, Heart-Master Da picked up one of the vows and looked at it closely for a long time. Then He nodded and put it down. He repeated this with each vow—looking at each one very carefully. I knew then that there was no going back!

This vow is a very strict way to live, very disciplined. But we live in Satsang[1] with Love-Ananda and that is the Happiness of the Brahmacharya life. We all know from our own experience what it is like to live without really practicing, just doing things because you are told to and not really wanting to and always resisting it. That is just suffering—it makes your life un-Happy and difficult. Everything feels like a problem then. But we live the discipline because we know that it makes our life truly Happy and that this is the way that we want to live. Even if we do not get to do all of the things that we want to do, it is a much Happier way to live. We love Sat-Guru Da very much. We really value the Teaching and the Guidance that He Gives us. So we take this vow very seriously.

Some people have asked, "How binding is it?" Well, it is completely binding. "Binding" is not exactly the right word for it, because that sounds kind of forced. It is not forced. We are happy to be able to choose it. But the brahmacharya vow is never to be broken, ever. It outlines all of our practices, so it is a very important agreement to keep. It is a vow to Heart-Master Da Love-Ananda, our Hridaya-Samartha Sat-Guru.

The Dreamworld of my Downfall

by Brahmacharini Naamleela

Our relationship to Heart-Master Da is very formal but it is also very Happy. In some ways that relationship is very Blessing and demanding, and in other ways it is very Blessing and enjoyable. It is demanding when we have to tell Him why we got the food discipline or something like that. But it is also very enjoyable because He is very Compassionate. He knows that we can't be perfect. We also bring to Him not just un-Happy things that we have done wrong but also Happy things that we have done. He always wants to know if there was something very enjoyable and special that we did that day.

Last year (1988) when Heart-Master Da was on His Tour of Blessing, we visited Tumomama Sanctuary on Kauai. While we were there, we read an article about a special natural ice-cream place that had opened on the island. It sounded very good! One day when we were coming back from a beach trip with Heart-Master Da, the car turned in a different direction. We were going to the ice-cream parlor as a surprise.

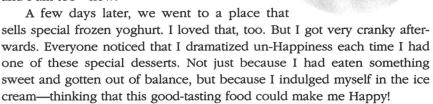

It turned out to be a nice place—but the best thing was the ice cream. I really liked it. I took my ice cream into a corner and ate it completely by myself. I didn't want anything to distract me from this great dessert! Everybody was very amused, and I am too—now.

A few days later, we went to a place that sells special frozen yoghurt. I loved that, too. But I got very cranky afterwards. Everyone noticed that I dramatized un-Happiness each time I had one of these special desserts. Not just because I had eaten something sweet and gotten out of balance, but because I indulged myself in the ice cream—thinking that this good-tasting food could make me Happy!

I had to make an agreement before we went to another ice-cream place that I would not dramatize after eating dessert. But I dramatized again after we left the restaurant. As a consequence, when one of my teeth came out a few days later, I couldn't have the usual special "tooth treat". I had to learn that food doesn't make you Happy—not even great desserts. In fact, you can get very un-Happy if you don't remember to practice during and after having special treats. You cannot just indulge yourself. Heart-Master Da still reminds me of this. He calls the way I get distracted by desserts "the dreamworld of my downfall", and He uses occasions of enjoyment (like having special desserts) to Teach us important Spiritual lessons.

Heart-Master Da has found many ways to Teach us that, even though life can be full of ordinary pleasures like good ice cream, real Happiness comes before anything that you can do or eat or enjoy or lose. In *Look at the Sunlight on the Water*, a book He has written about how to raise children, He says,

Every child must be free and ecstatic at the simple native level of his or her own existence. Every child must be awakened to feel that he is associated with an Infinite Power or Mystery that sustains him, that gave him birth, that is his

Destiny, and that is the Power that moves his entire future if he will associate with It rightly.[1]

Parents and teachers tend to think that they must constantly be stimulating young people, constantly providing ways to entertain them through field trips, sporting activities, and so on. They think that every day, for significant periods of time, they need to somehow interrupt the cycle of discipline, of peacefulness, ease, and naturalness, with stimulations that permit young people to indulge outgoing exuberance, the vital motive, or bondage to their conventional tendencies of attention. . . .

This is a renunciate Way of life. It is a spiritual Way of life. It involves the free, intelligent discipline of functional existence, not its suppression. There can be occasional amusements—all the pleasures of existence are potential in such a disciplined Way of life. But its principle is spiritual in nature, and its practice is characterized by equanimity.[2]

So, there are many very enjoyable things in our life with Heart-Master Da Love-Ananda, and He Gives all these pleasurable things to us in balance with the rest of our brahmacharya discipline. He Gives them in relationship to our whole Way of life so that they fit in and so that they strengthen our practice.

**Heart-Master Da Love-Ananda with the Hridaya Da Gurukula
at Golden Gate Park, San Francisco, 1989**

What Is an Idiosyncrasy?

by Brahmacharini Tamarind

One day in April, Kanya Navaneeta (who is my Kanya guide) was speaking with Heart-Master Da Love-Ananda about my practice. She told Him that she had noticed that if I was getting a cold and one side of my nose was stuffed up or I was not breathing freely, I did not like to be touched. If she was being affectionate with me, putting her hand on my knee or something like that, I would move her hand away because I did not like how it felt. I would get nervous about people touching me because I thought I might get even sicker.

Kanya Navaneeta

He called this habit of mine an idiosyncrasy and He began to Give me some Instruction about how to practice with this habit.

HEART-MASTER DA LOVE-ANANDA: There are some Yogic principles and principles of health that are good to maintain. Whatever Tamarind is doing to maintain her health according to these principles is good. But it should be pointed out to her that it is possible for a person to get very self-protective and obsessed with doing things correctly and obsessed with avoiding contact with unpleasant things like germs. If you become obsessed with such rituals, you become mechanical and you dissociate from other people and from physical life.

You must be mindful of any such habits that you are developing. You should discuss them with other practitioners and discover what the reason for your developing such habits might be. Usually an emotional stress is the underlying cause. But whatever the underlying problem or anxiety or fear is, it should be dealt with directly, rather than creating a ritual around it.

The Kanyas should also observe the other three Brahmacharinis and see if they have likewise developed some of these habits. Some such habits may be generally all right, but they should never be obsessive. Each Brahmacharini should discuss with her Kanya guide what her anxious, ritual behaviors might be. Each should have a list of these habits and discuss the conditions they could take on to systematically release such behaviors.

He also asked us to keep track of our lists of these habits until the habits had changed. So that afternoon, we started a very useful exercise. First, we had a meeting with Kanya Remembrance. After reading Heart-Master Da's Instructions to us, she had us each write out a list of all the different ways that we acted out these anxiety rituals. Some of the things we did were very ridiculous or superstitious—like trying to ensure a good night's sleep by straightening everybody's shoes before going to bed. We had to laugh at some of our habits! Then we read our lists out loud to each other and discussed why we did these things. After that conversation, we saw how unnecessary our habits were, and so we stopped doing them.

We continued writing things down when we noticed something that we did as a habit. Our friends and teachers helped us, too. They wrote things down that they noticed us doing as well. Several days later, on Sunday, our retreat day, we had another meeting and we rewrote our lists, adding any new habits that we had observed. We also wrote out why we did them, what the feeling behind each habit was. We also wrote about the habits we had released that week and how it felt to not do these rituals anymore. Then we gave our lists to Heart-Master Da Love-Ananda.

After we took responsibility for our habits and released them, we noticed that we had a lot more free attention for our practice. It was easier to Contemplate Heart-Master Da Love-Ananda and let go of worrying and being anxious. Now, if we happen to notice any habits like this (or if anybody else notices us doing something like this) we discuss why we did it and we release the habit.

"I Am Not Interested in Anything but Six!"

by Brahmacharini Shawnee

L ast year (1989), a month or two after we re-stated our brahmacharya vows, Heart-Master Da Love-Ananda went on a tour of Blessing to see His devotees in other parts of the world. He traveled first to The Mountain Of Attention Hermitage Ashram in northern California, and all of the Kanyas and all of us, the Brahmacharinis, traveled with Him.

Many things had changed for us. Before the "honey incident" and all the important lessons that followed it, I practiced by living as Heart-Master Da recommends most of the time. But, as you know very well by now, I did not always agree with the discipline, and I took advantage of opportunities to indulge myself. In fact, I was often trying to get out of the demand of practice in one way or another. I loved Heart-Master Da and took my practice seriously, but I was not completely committed. Practicing Happiness was not the only reason I was alive.

So even though I got those lessons because I was not practicing, now I am glad that it all occurred the way it did. I feel very grateful for Heart-Master Da's Instruction and how He Helped me to feel that the Way to grow in Happiness Itself is by feeling Him and resorting to Him. Here is an example of how giving feeling and attention to Heart-Master Da has helped me.

Every time that He travels to The Mountain Of Attention, Heart-Master Da Love-Ananda goes to Ordeal Bath Lodge, a healing site that He has Blessed and filled with His Happiness. Ordeal Bath Lodge is a large bath house with many rooms containing baths fed by natural hot springs. It is full of greenery and light and steam from the hot, healing waters. It also contains a fair-sized indoor swimming pool.

Over the years, each time we visit The Mountain Of Attention and Ordeal Bath Lodge, I have practiced swimming underwater in the pool. I would do laps underwater without breathing, seeing how long I could go before I would have to take a breath. Heart-Master Da Love-Ananda would watch me and ask me to keep going, to learn to do more laps. He has done fifteen laps without taking a breath, which amazes me because it is not a short pool.

This year I tried again. My record from my previous visit had been five laps. So, naturally, I tried to break my record and do six. But I was struggling, unable to do it. On one particular day, Heart-Master Da Love-Ananda watched me. I could only do four. I kept breaking off my laps and coming up early for breath.

Heart-Master Da Love-Ananda finally said to me, "I am not interested in anything but six!"

"Oh. Uh-oh," I responded, somewhat uncertain that I could do it. He challenged me, "I want to see six—right now!"

So I went to the edge of the pool and took a deep breath. I knew I had to take a different approach this time. I decided I would relax and Contemplate Heart-Master Da Love-Ananda while I was swimming. I let go of all my feelings of struggling and failing and put my attention on feeling Him. I dove into the water and started doing laps. Sure enough, before too long, I started to feel the hurt of wanting to breathe. I started to contract and get anxious, thinking that I was going to have to take a breath immediately—otherwise I thought I was going to die. But then I remembered what I was going to do differently this time. I started Contemplating Heart-Master Da Love-Ananda and "breathing" His Happiness with my feeling.

I could still feel the hurt of wanting to breathe air with my lungs, but I noticed that I had been identifying with the pain. I had been feeling that "I" _was_ the hurt and the feeling of need. Now, I just "stood back" from the feeling of struggle and need and I Contemplated Heart-Master Da instead. I could still feel the hurt, but my attention was not on it anymore. My attention was on Heart-Master Da Love-Ananda and the Happy Feeling of Who He Is. The pain did not matter to me anymore. So, I just kept swimming. I did six laps, and when I came up, Heart-Master Da Love-Ananda was clapping (and so was everybody else). It was a very difficult thing for me to do, and I was a little dizzy, but I smiled at Heart-Master Da. He smiled at me and nodded and I knew that I had received His Blessing and the great Gift of right relationship to Him. Because of this, I finally did six! So I have learned that if you live in Satsang with Heart-Master Da Love-Ananda, it makes your whole life Happy. If you live Satsang with Him, you are Happy if you are sweeping the floor or if you are eating an ice-cream cone. Obviously, you might still prefer to eat an ice-cream cone—but no matter which one you are doing, you are still Happy. Even if you are doing something that you don't want to do, you can still be Happy.

Satsang is the enjoyment of our brahmacharya practice. But this enjoyment is also available to everyone. I know this is true. When I was living in the village, I did not see Heart-Master Da Love-Ananda except for the rare occasions when He walked to the library. But it was one of the Happiest times of my whole life—because I was living the discipline of practice because I wanted to. I really enjoyed it, and I could really feel Da Love-Ananda. I started to see the Wisdom behind why Heart-Master Da has asked me to do all of the brahmacharya disciplines. I could see that it was not to deprive me in any way. During my time in the village, I did not do things that you would usually call "fun". My life was very strict. But I was Happy. I could see that if I really did these disciplines as a means of remaining in Satsang with my Heart-Master, I was really Happy more and more.

I am very grateful for everything that Heart-Master Da Love-Ananda and the Kanyas and all of my friends have given to me. I am particularly grateful for the brahmacharya discipline. I really appreciate it, because it is a Happy Way to live.

The Brahmacharinis after the third annual ceremony affirming
their Brahmacharya vow, May 4, 1990.
Left to right: Brahmacharini Tamarind, age 14; Brahmacharini Shawnee, age 14;
Brahmacharini Naamleela, age 10; Brahmacharini Io, age 14

THE GIFT OF THE SPIRIT

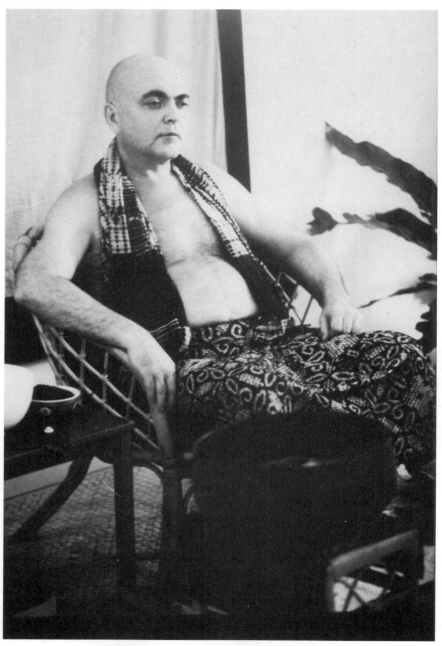

**Heart-Master Da Love-Ananda Granting Darshan
at Taken To Heart, May 9, 1990**

Taken To Heart

by Brahmacharini Shawnee

One day this year (1990), not long after the third anniversary of our Upanayana ceremony, I was sitting at my desk, hard at work on an English grammar assignment. It seemed to be an ordinary day in the Ashram. There was a clear sky and a light breeze. Everything was lively but in order—calm and usual. I stood up from work and walked up the hill to another classroom.

Suddenly, Brahmacharini Io came running up.

"Brahmacharini Shawnee!" she shouted, "Love-Ananda just walked into the dining room while the devotees on retreat were in there chanting! He was all by Himself—even the Kanyas, who <u>always</u> attend Him when He goes to Darshan, weren't with Him! He's Sitting with the retreatants! He's Giving His Darshan!"

Well, Heart-Master Da Love-Ananda has always Moved Freely and I have seen many of His spontaneous and even surprising Gestures, but this was totally unexpected!

Brahmacharini Io continued her amazing story, "The retreatants were chanting, just like they always do at this time of day, when, suddenly,

Love-Ananda was Standing there in front of them! Everyone was so surprised, they stopped chanting. The room went completely silent!"

I could just see it happening: What an incredible Surprise that would be—to have Heart-Master Da appear in front of you so unexpectedly!

"He sat down and right now He is Giving Darshan!"

The ecstatic noises of devotees responding to their Heart-Master soon confirmed what she had told me. Their Happy shout could be heard all the way across the Ashram from Taken To Heart, the dining room where Heart-Master Da was Sitting with them. I was very excited.

Darshan occasions are formal times when Heart-Master Da Love-Ananda Grants His Blessing to devotees in a very special way, by Sitting with them in Silence and allowing them to feel how He is always Radiating His Love and Freedom and Happiness to everyone.

Because they are so special, Darshan occasions are almost always well planned: they are usually formally announced to everyone, Prasad[1] is specially made in advance, flowers are put along Heart-Master Da Love-Ananda's path, and everyone has to be seated at least half an hour before He is expected to arrive.

Heart-Master Da Love-Ananda has Given His Darshan Blessing in many other ways as well. Sometimes He will invite devotees to greet Him when He returns from a trip to another part of Sri Love-Anandashram. At those times, He has Given us His Darshan by Standing Still for all to feel and see Him. Sometimes He Stands near Ralph Royce (the Land Rover He rides in), sometimes He Stands in the middle of the lawn, sometimes He Stands near the porch of Indefinable (His house in the village). And He has, at times, invited devotees to gather around His front porch so that He can Sit with them and Grant His Darshan there.

But even these more spontaneous occasions are not as surprising as this day—devotees generally know He is coming beforehand and have at least a few minutes to prepare before He comes.

Heart-Master Da Love-Ananda is an Avadhoot, which is a Sanskrit title that means He has Shaken off all un-Happiness and He is Free. He does not have to do anything in order to Be Happy—He already IS Happiness itself! Because of this, Heart-Master Da does only what His Freedom and His Divine Mission of Blessing Move Him to Do. Even so, Darshan is not usually a complete surprise . . . at least not up until today!

As Brahmacharini Io talked, I remembered Darshan occasions I had been to before. I remembered seeing Heart-Master Da Love-Ananda Sitting Silent with His Eyes closed or open Wide with Bliss. I remembered seeing tears of Ecstasy roll down His Cheeks and watching His Hands

Move in Beautiful Gestures of Divine Blessing, moving the hearts of all those present as They Danced. I remembered seeing that His Feet Dance Blissfully, too. As I remembered all this, I felt that there is nothing in the world as Happy as Heart-Master Da's Darshan.

I ran to tell the other Brahmacharinis. Everyone was laughing and smiling and telling the story to one another over and over again. Questions like, "What is happening down there?" and "Aren't those retreatants lucky?" clearly showed how much everyone longed to be in Taken To Heart with Him.

But we had not been invited. So, instead, we sat down and tried to concentrate on our music lesson. This was just about the last thing I wanted to do just then!

Hardly had we begun, when we heard the steady beating of the lali drum—a loud Fijian drum in the middle of the village which is the special signal that means everyone is invited to Darshan!

I leapt up, shaking with joy! We all ran out the door before we had time to think about what we were doing. We were told to get musical instruments and run to Taken To Heart at top speed. We certainly did not need to be told to run—we practically flew! As we neared Taken To Heart, we could hear chanting, mixed with all kinds of other ecstatic shouts and cries. We stood outside the door, longing to go in, but unsure we should interrupt by opening the door.

We did not have to wait long. Another devotee, bolder than we were, rushed past us and burst through the door. We, of course, crowded in after her.

A blast of noise and Energy instantly surrounded me. An incredible, Blissful Energy swept down the front of my body and I felt its heat all over. I felt rooted to the floor by this Energy pushing down into my body and I started to tremble with the Force. I tried to hold off

"A blast of noise and Energy instantly surrounded me."

this Energy until I could find a space where I would be able to see Heart-Master Da in the midst of all the devotees gathered so close around Him.

Heart-Master Da Love-Ananda was Sitting in His Chair at the front of the room, Radiating a Tremendous "Bright" Energy to everyone. Everyone was captured by His Beauty and the Force of His Blessing. Devotees were sitting, standing, kneeling—many were chanting, some were weeping wildly at the sight of the God-Man Da Sitting before them, and others were calling out in ecstasy. Some were meditating silently in the midst of this Blissful madness!

I started playing the tambourine with the chanters and musicians. People were pressing in on me—on all sides I was surrounded (and even squashed!) by devotees singing in my ears, rocking me (and everyone else!) back and forth with their wild, ecstatic motions. It seemed chaotic, but I knew what was happening to everyone.

Can you imagine what it would feel like to walk into a room and see Someone Who Is completely and absolutely Happy? Totally Free? Obviously Blissful with the Force of Absolute Divinity? Perfectly Alive as Love in Person? Can you imagine what it would be like to behold the Infinite Mysterious Divine Being in a human Form?

Here before us was such a One. Heart-Master Da Love-Ananda was Blessing everyone with the Power and the Blissfulness of the Mystery Itself. This Power is so Immense that it dissolves un-Happiness in an instant, leaving nothing but Joy.

But even though I knew this, I began to feel a little self-conscious, noticing, "These people have really let loose!" I could feel everyone responding to the Power of His Blessing. I looked back at Heart-Master Da Love-Ananda. His face was contorted with Ecstasy. It reminded me of the Bliss-Wounded expression I had seen on His face so many years ago when I felt the Mystery at the Love of the God-Man Celebration.

Now, I remembered what I experienced in Darshan that day in 1984: It happened almost instantly, as soon as I gave Heart-Master Da Love-Ananda my attention. Everything dissolved. "I" dissolved. There was nothing there but Vast, Incredible Being. There was no time or space. I could only see Heart-Master Da Love-Ananda with His Hands held motionless in the most Beautiful Gestures of Blessing. I could not see or hear any of the hundreds of devotees chanting and dancing all around me. I could not even feel my body. There was not anything or anyone left to feel these things with. "I" was not "me". I seemed to be the whole universe. I was looking at Heart-Master Da Love-Ananda, but at the same time I <u>was</u> Heart-Master Da Love-Ananda. There was not the slightest separation from Him or anything. There were no limits or boundaries to anything. I did not have a mind. There was no "me" to have one. I could not feel "my" body. It felt like I was doing exactly what He was doing—my body was like a mirror, but there was still no separation. He took over my body with His Blessing Force and moved it as Him. I sat there in complete and total ecstasy.

The Love of the God-Man Celebration, 1984

I have no idea how long this lasted. Suddenly, another devotee danced in front of me, blocking my view of Heart-Master Da Love-Ananda. I looked around me. Everyone else was standing up dancing and clapping to the chant. I stood up, still feeling this limitless Deep even though I was now conscious of my body.

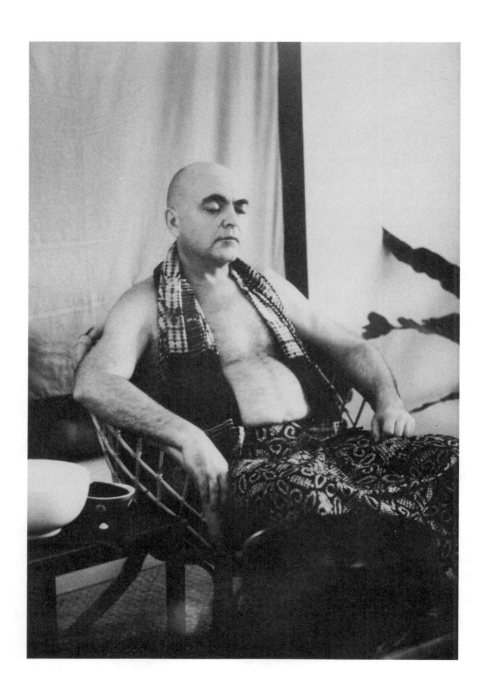

After some time, Heart-Master Da Love-Ananda left the tent. I noticed that I had been crying. After a few hours, the Unlimited Feeling He had Given me began to fade even though I really tried to hold on to it.

Now I was feeling Him that strongly for the first time since then. And I was also feeling His Blessing in a new way—His Spirit-Power was coming into my body and filling me with His Joy.

Suddenly, I felt the Energy I had first felt when I entered the room rush into my body even more strongly. Now I could not resist. I let myself go, and the Energy magnified instantly. It ran through my muscles so powerfully that it made them shake violently. My whole body was quivering.

This was Heart-Master Da Love-Ananda's Blissful Spirit-Energy, and it took over my whole body. I could not play the tambourine any more. I felt His Energy moving through my body more strongly than ever before. I started crying and screaming because It was so strong. I felt completely consumed. The Name "Da" was all around me—all the devotees were calling out to "Da". I found myself saying my Heart-Master's Name over and over, ecstatically. "Da!" "Da!" "Da!"

In the midst of this surrender and Blessing, I heard my mind feebly insisting that now I had gone mad, too. Here I was, screaming like a fool in front of all these people, having lost every remnant of self-consciousness! But that was the last I heard from my grumbling mind for some time. Its weak arguments were soon blotted out.

Heart-Master Da Love-Ananda's Force descended into my body until everything that I usually cling to was torn away. His Blessing was like a Great River that washed away everything in its path—all my un-Happiness and even my sense of being "me" were dissolved in His Love and Bliss.

Heart-Master Da Love-Ananda Looked out at everyone. He Looked directly at me. His Look was so fierce and strong and Compassionate that I knew He could undo everyone's un-Happiness. I felt like I was being pinned to the floor as His Spirit-Energy rushed into my body even more strongly.

He Blessed the Prasad by sprinkling it with water. Then He picked up the water bowl and began splashing everyone with water, Blessing the whole room! Now devotees really went mad with devotion (myself included this time)—weeping, yelling, singing, calling out His Name "Da!" "Da!" "Da!", "Om Sri Da Love-Ananda Hridayam!", making ecstatic gestures with their hands and faces and bodies. There was so much Blessing in the room it was impossible not to be swept away. Just as He was about to leave, Heart-Master Da Love-Ananda Smiled a Radiant Smile, to the delight of all His devotees.

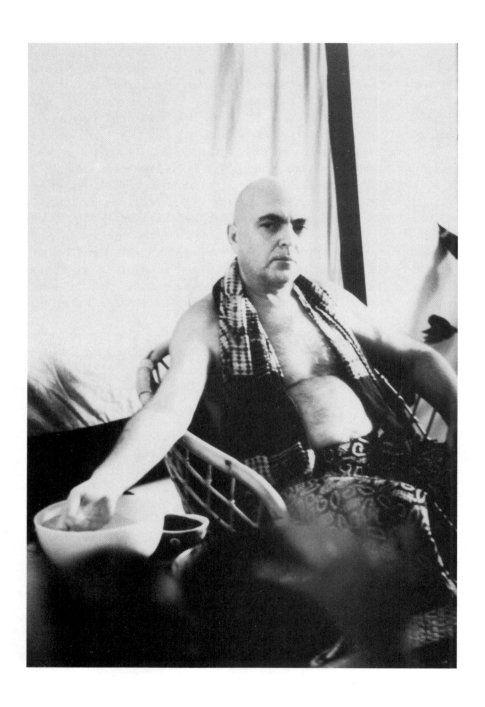

"He Blessed the Prasad by sprinkling it with water.
Then He picked up the water bowl
and began splashing everyone with water,
Blessing the whole room! Now devotees really went
mad with devotion (myself included this time)—
weeping, yelling, singing, calling out His Name
'Da!' 'Da!' 'Da!' 'Om Sri Da Love-Ananda Hridayam!',
making ecstatic gestures with their
hands and faces and bodies."

When Heart-Master Da left Taken To Heart, everyone followed Him out onto the lawn. He walked away toward Turtle Cove, a beautiful spot a short walk down the beach. All the devotees sat down and watched as He walked out of sight.

Now I felt myself getting a little hysterical, out of control in my usual sense. His Spirit-Energy seemed to be shooting out, spreading through my whole body as I sat on the lawn. I could not stop crying. Then I remembered that I had to relax and trust and really use this Gift of Spirit-Blessing that Heart-Master Da Love-Ananda was Giving me. I breathed very deeply. I did not "try" to stop crying, I simply practiced Contemplating Him in my feeling and I relaxed. I began to feel very blissful. I felt Heart-Master Da Love-Ananda fill and expand my heart with His Love. It was a spaceless, timeless ecstasy. I felt the Infinite Vastness of the Mystery.

Heart-Master Da Love-Ananda came walking back up the path. He looked so Beautiful! The sun was shining on His gourd hat. It is almost impossible to describe how He looked, because words are just too small! He was only the Heart.

He walked past us and disappeared into Indefinable. Everyone still sat, enraptured, unable to move.

As I sat there, I knew that this Happiness was the Secret that He had been telling me about. In the days and weeks that followed this event, I was so happy to notice that I could feel His Heart-Blessing and Happiness anywhere, at any time—if I only Remembered Him. Unlike my experience of His Blessing at the Love of the God-Man Celebration, this was not a one-time experience.

Because Heart-Master Da Love-Ananda had shown me the importance of devotion, service, self-discipline, and meditation, and because He had Given me the strength to go beyond my limits, I could receive His real Secret. Now, He had Revealed to me What was beyond those limits—His Truth, Freedom, Perfect Happiness, and Immense Joy! And He had Given me all the means I needed to allow His Grace into my heart forever.

Now that you and I have both heard about the Two Secrets, we have started a conversation that we can keep having for a long, long time. There are so many more Stories that I could tell you about Heart-Master Da Love-Ananda and His Great Gifts of Blessing—and I will! There are many books to write describing and praising His Heart-Blessing, but I am very happy that I could begin with this one. Because now we can both celebrate His Secret about Happiness with one another and with everyone else, too! And, really, celebrating Happiness is the best and truest and only everlasting thing we could ever do!

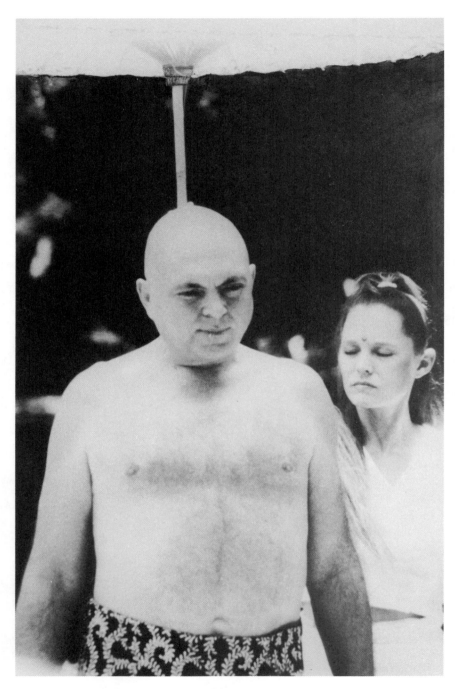

**Kanya Remembrance attends Heart-Master Da Love-Ananda
during a Darshan occasion**

Tending the Fire
Now and Always

In the ancient brahmacharya schools, each morning before beginning the day's instruction students would fetch wood for the sacred fire
that the Guru would light that day. They were also often given the
responsibility to tend the Guru's sacred fire—keeping the flames alive.
When they did this, they knew that they were performing an all-
important function—they were supporting the Guru's work and acting as
an inspiring sign to all those who came to the Guru for help. As the
brahmacharis grew, they would be given many other responsibilities for
serving the work of the Guru, but they learned that responsibility first by
fetching firewood and feeding the sacred fire.

The four Brahmacharinis of Sri Love-Anandashram are learning a
similar responsibility. Heart-Master Da Love-Ananda has told the Brahmacharinis that they are being prepared to tend the Fire of His Sacred
and World-Transforming Work, carrying it into future generations.

It is Heart-Master Da Love-Ananda's Intention that, by His Grace,
they will all one day be strong enough in the discipline of Happiness to
serve as what He calls "Instruments" of His Great Work. Such Instruments, simply by the force and example of their own self-transcending

devotion to Heart-Master Da, inspire others to feel and receive His Gifts of Heart-Awakening Grace.

And, ultimately, the Brahmacharinis may even serve as fully Awakened "Agents" of His Work. Such Agents are Enlightened devotees who have Realized the Living God and who live in unbroken Communion with the One Mysterious Reality that is Alive as everyone. Because their self-forgetting Happiness in feeling-Contemplation of Heart-Master Da has become Perfect, they become living human conduits of His Heart-Transmission to others. When they eventually qualify to perform this Service, the Brahmacharinis will be the first to follow the Kanyadana Kumaris in a sacred line of devotees who will tend the Fire of His Universal Blessing Work forever.

The Brahmacharinis (or any devotee who may grow to serve as one of Heart-Master Da's Instruments or Agents) will always be devoted to Heart-Master Da Love-Ananda (and will never become teachers or "Awakeners" independent of their relationship to Him). Heart-Master Da Love-Ananda has the unique Blessing Function as Hridaya-Samartha Sat-Guru. That Function is Eternal, and no one can ever stand in His Place. But His most mature devotees will provide a living link to Heart-Master Da for all future devotees in the Way of the Heart.

The four Kanyadanas are the first to provide that link. Through their own example of what it looks and feels like to be made Happy by devotion to Heart-Master Da, they inspire all others to grow in their practice of the Way of the Heart. Heart-Master Da has prepared the Kanyas for this service for many, many years. Here Kanya Suprithi praises the Gift of practice she has been Given:

If I did what I was supposed to do with responsibility and simply Contemplated His bodily (human) Form, His Spiritual (and Always Blessing) Presence, and His Very (and Inherently Perfect) State, the process was Revealed. I have devoted my life to Sri Gurudev Da Love-Ananda for the sake of Perfect Awakening, and I have learned that the process can advance very quickly, but being patient and a steady practitioner was the first step.

I feel it is also important to address all practitioners as well as the entire world of people today to say how vital it is for the sake of individuals, as well as for the sake of mankind, not to take lightly the Offering that Heart-Master Da Gives to all beings.

I am certain that all that Sri Gurudev Da Love-Ananda has Said in His Written Teachings is the Living Truth, and I am certain of His Liberating Ability and Power.

All beings would do well to witness the authenticity of a Spiritual Master of the Ultimate Degree in this day and age, when millions of people profoundly suffer the lack of direct contact with God.

I hope for the sake of all mankind that they have the opportunity to hear Heart-Master Da's Words and be thereby moved by heart to receive what they have always been searching for.

All the Kanyadana Kumaris work together to support the heart-practice of the four Brahmacharinis. In addition, each of the Brahmacharinis is apprenticed to one of the Kanyas to learn the art of devotion and to learn about the many responsibilities that she will assume in the future.

And so it is that the Gurukula that surrounds Heart-Master Da consists of two inspiring Circles of devotion that serve to magnify His Blessing to everyone. Because of this, all Free Daists happily support and serve the inspirational work of The Hridaya Da Gurukula Kanyadana Kumari Mandala, and we also serve the members of The Hridaya Da Gurukula Brahmacharini Mandala so that they, too, will grow to be of great service to the sacred culture and the world even beyond Heart-Master Da's lifetime.

Just as the Kanyas and the Brahmacharinis practice intensely not only for their own sake, but for the sake of making Heart-Master Da's Blessing available to everyone now and into the future, you should know that you are also called to respond to Him as fully as you can. For His Blessings Freely flow to you and to everyone.

Heart-Master Da looks every day to see who is interested in True Happiness and who will make use of His Blessing, and He is always at Work to Grow that Happiness in anyone who responds to Him. His devotees have observed this for many, many years and we know it to be True beyond all doubting. And He has also Shown us that He does not do this for just a few—He does it for you and for everyone, everywhere, all the time. That is why He is the World-Teacher.

It is our prayer that, by reading the story of *The Two Secrets (yours, and Mine)*, you will feel the Happiness that Heart-Master Da Love-Ananda Is and also that you will be moved to make use of the Wisdom and Blessing that He Offers. In fact, all of the Kanyadana Kumaris and Brahmacharinis extend Heart-Master Da's Invitation to you. Kanya Tripura Rahasya describes how Heart-Master Da Love-Ananda's Grace Flows to all:

Heart-Master Da Love-Ananda's Appearance in this world surpasses anything that has ever existed in the manifest worlds. He is not merely

Working with individuals, He is Working with and Blessing the entire world. He is here to perform the Great Function of Divine World-Teacher, to bring the Divine to all beings, not to a thousand people, not to one, not to two, not to a small group of people, not just to those who already are His formally acknowledged devotees. His Divine Grace Flows to the heart of anyone who will receive it. Come to Him to forget your "self" in the Ecstasy of His Greatness. Such Ecstasy is absolutely available to all. Once you enter formally into the sacred relationship with Him, His Grace is utterly present.

Heart-Master Da also always looks for those whose response is most strong and who will prepare themselves to serve His Great World-Work of Heart-Blessing in the future.

Kanya Navaneeta calls you to feel your own response to His Great Heart-Offering:

Truly, I can confess to you that it is possible for anyone to grow in the Way of the Heart simply by obedience and surrender to Sat-Guru Da Love-Ananda. It does not matter how difficult your physical or emotional or mental tendencies may be, because His Transforming Power is Absolute. His Grace is Boundless. But you must surrender to receive Him. Do not waste His Gifts by clinging to self. Do not withdraw from the Great Fire of His Demand by consoling yourself. Do not flee from His Tapas by turning from Him. Do not be complacent, in the face of His Urgency, by counting on time. His physical Incarnation is brief, a Blessing Incomparable. Da Avadhoota is the Hridaya-Samartha Sat-Guru, Who Can Liberate you. May you be Blessed to respond to Heart-Master Da Love-Ananda Hridayam with great devotion.

May you be made Happy by the discovery of His Secret and may you be moved to accept the Blessings that so freely flow to you (and all) through and in and as Heart-Master Da Love-Ananda.

OM SRI DA LOVE-ANANDA HRIDAYAM

Heart-Master Da Love-Ananda leaving a Darshan occasion

Taking Up Brahmacharya Practice in the Way of the Heart

T he four Brahmacharinis in this book live a wonderful, ancient (meaning traditionally honored), and new (because the Way of the Heart is unique) Way of life established by Heart-Master Da Love-Ananda for those who would grow strong in Happiness. But they are not the only ones for whom this is a possibility.

The original Hridaya Da Gurukula Brahmacharini Mandala will always remain unique and distinct within our Communion. However, the Gift of brahmacharya practice that Heart-Master Da Love-Ananda extends to them is also His Offering to all young devotees who qualify for and enter The (Free Daist) Lay Brahmacharya Order, just as it is also a model of Wisdom for children and young people throughout the world.

All children and young people who respond to Heart-Master Da's Gifts of Happiness and who have embraced the Way of the Heart take up brahmacharya practice and eventually apply for formal membership in The (Free Daist) Lay Brahmacharya Order. This Order is a Gift from Heart-Master Da to all His young devotees so that they may dedicate a specified period of their life to the most intensive and one-pointed practice of the brahmacharya discipline. Young people in The (Free Daist) Lay Brahmacharya Order continue the brahmacharya discipline until they are twenty-five, unless at age twenty-one or beyond they feel (with appropriate and formal cultural guidance) that an intimate relationship is an auspicious choice or if they enter either The Lay Congregationist Order or The Lay Renunciate Order of The Free Daist Communion. Members of The (Free Daist) Lay Brahmacharya Order may begin to "consider" the possibility of an emotional-sexual intimacy as early as age twenty-one, if they qualify as prepared student-beginners in the Way of the Heart.

Taking up brahmacharya practice is a very Happy choice, but it is also an extremely serious one. Brahmacharis must know with their hearts that they want to devote their lives to the practice of Happiness that Heart-Master Da Reveals to all. In accepting a brahmachari into the Order, Heart-Master Da Offers the Gift of His Heart-Blessing and His Guidance. All brahmacharis in the Way of the Heart respond to that Perfect Gift through their practice of devotion, service, self-discipline, and meditation, exactly as they are Instructed to do by their Brahmacharya Master, Heart-Master Da Love-Ananda. To ask Heart-Master Da for acceptance into the Order is to make a lifetime vow of practice of the Way of the Heart. (Even if, at some appropriate point, a brahmachari chooses to relinquish his or her membership in the Brahmacharya Order to choose an intimate partner, he or she would continue to practice in the context of the greater culture of all practitioners in the Way of the Heart.) What else could a true devotee—either as a brahmachari or as an adult practitioner—do but live and practice with great joy, and always renewed gratitude, at the Feet of his or her Heart-Master?

Heart-Master Da has outlined the form of preparation required of applicants to The (Free Daist) Lay Brahmacharya Order. Because the brahmacharya commitment is such a serious one, young people (and their families) should use these qualifications to measure their readiness to make such a formal commitment and to know what steps they should take to prepare further:

❖ Brahmacharis in The (Free Daist) Lay Brahmacharya Order gratefully accept Heart-Master Da's Guidance and Help as their Brahmacharya Master.

❖ Anyone who enters The (Free Daist) Lay Brahmacharya Order must understand that he or she has many requirements and responsibilities to fulfill.

❖ Because of the circumstance that must be created and maintained by the community of devotees to make brahmacharya practice possible, and because of the great and Spiritually intimate Service that Heart-Master Da provides for brahmacharya practitioners, brahmacharis enter into a lifetime bond with Heart-Master Da Love-Ananda and the sacred community of His devotees. Anyone who enters The (Free Daist) Lay Brahmacharya Order must understand this and be willing to maintain commitment to practice throughout his or her adult life, even after the period of brahmacharya is completed.

❖ The parents of young brahmacharya practitioners must themselves be mature and stable practitioners of the Way of the Heart. (Parents who do not meet this requirement but who support the commitment to brahmacharya practice made by their children can, by mutual cultural agreement, make boarding arrangements with other mature practitioners of the Way of the Heart, who consent to provide for the personal care and cultural guidance of their children.)

All applicants to The (Free Daist) Lay Brahmacharya Order must be accepted Personally by Heart-Master Da Love-Ananda during His physical human Lifetime, or by a practitioner of the Way of the Heart whom Heart-Master Da has appointed to provide such formal acceptance.

To take up brahmacharya practice in the Way of the Heart is a great honor and a great Gift. But everyone, no matter how young or old, how near or far, is very welcome to respond to Heart-Master Da Love-Ananda's Blessing. There are many forms of participation in the "Hard School and Happy Way of life" that He Offers, for Heart-Master Da Love-Ananda Freely Extends His Blessing to all.

If you are interested in finding out more about the unique system of schooling in the Way of the Heart, please contact us at this address:

The Free Daist Brahmacharya School
12060 Shenandoah Road
Middletown, CA 95461
USA
(707) 928-5640

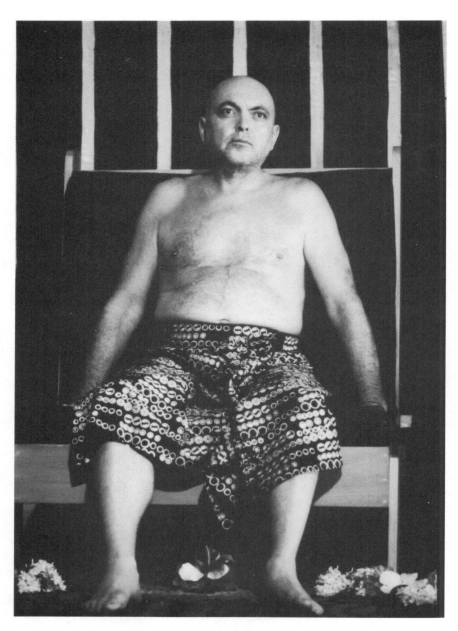

Heart-Master Da Love-Ananda, 1990

The Unique Advantage of the God-Man

An Invitation from The Free Daist Communion

Of all the means for Spiritual growth and the Realization of Divine Happiness that have been offered in the many sacred traditions of humankind throughout history, the most especially treasured is the Way of Satsang—which is the Way lived in the Blessing Company of One Who has Realized Truth, Freedom, and Happiness Itself.

Heart-Master Da Love-Ananda Offers this prized and Graceful Opportunity to everyone—through the uniquely Perfect Medium of His own Incarnation as the Divine Person. His unprecedented Emergence as World-Teacher, the One predicted and expected since ancient times, has made the Universal Blessing Power of the Divine most directly available in our time and for all time to come.

Heart-Master Da has summarized His Offering of Satsang as follows:

What is supremely Attractive in the manifest universe and in the human world is the God-Man. All beings, male or female, must become Attracted, or Distracted, by that One. This is the Ultimate Means, the Supreme Means, the Supreme Yoga. It is for this reason that the Divine appears in manifest form in the likeness of those who are to be drawn out of bondage—but only in their likeness. *It is the* Divine *Who appears in that likeness, and it is the* Divine *Who is made visible through that likeness. Those who become capable of acknowledging that One become capable of responding to that Attraction. Those who become capable of being Distracted by that One become participants in this Supreme Way, which truly is the Way of Grace, because it requires no effort at all. It requires nothing but Grace and the response to Grace. That response is not effortful. It is easy. It is easy to respond to what is Attractive.*

To those who are interested in taking up this Blessed and transformative relationship to Him as Hridaya-Samartha Sat-Guru, Heart-Master Da Love-Ananda Offers the Way of the Heart. Practice of the Way of the Heart is the means for everyone to participate in and ultimately Realize the Divine Mystery that He Reveals.

Those who take up the Way of the Heart as Heart-Master Da Love-Ananda's devotees are given a whole new Way of life—a Happy and disciplined Way of life that offers many cherished sacred opportunities that support self-transcending practice, including participation in a community and a sacred culture of other practitioners. Through the devotional relationship to Heart-Master Da Love-Ananda and through responsible participation in the life of practice that He has Provided, everyone can learn to release the un-Happy patterns of the ego and enjoy the Feeling-Realization of the Mystery or God or Happiness instead.

Many, many people have been moved to take up the practice of the Way of the Heart, as you too may be—now or in the future. But many others are very grateful simply to benefit from Heart-Master Da Love-Ananda's Wisdom and Blessing by reading His Teaching literature and supporting His Heart-Awakening Work. The Free Daist Communion, which is the formal gathering of all Heart-Master Da Love-Ananda's devotees, offers many forms of association with His Universal Blessing Work. Whatever level of involvement and response you choose, it is our sacred task to make the Satsang that Heart-Master Da Offers available to you.

If you would like to receive a free introductory brochure or talk to a practicing devotee about forms of participation in the Way of the Heart, please write or call our Correspondence Department at this address:

Correspondence Department
The Free Daist Communion
P.O. Box 3680
Clearlake, California 95422
USA
Phone: (707) 928-4936

Notes to the Text

INTRODUCTION

1. The World-Teacher, Heart-Master Da Love-Ananda, *What and Where and Who To Remember To Be Happy: A Simple Explanation Of The Way Of The Heart (For Children, and Everyone Else)*, New Standard Edition. Forthcoming.

2. Adapted for children from a talk by Heart-Master Da Love-Ananda Given in November 1973.

3. Da Free John [Heart-Master Da Love-Ananda], *The Dreaded Gom-Boo, or the Imaginary Disease That Religion Seeks to Cure* (Clearlake, Calif.: The Dawn Horse Press, 1983), p. 364.

4. An Ashram is a place where a Spiritual Master lives (or has lived) with devotees. Ashrams may be established in the country or in the city, or in any place where the Spiritual Master chooses to live or where devotees live together to practice in relationship to their Spiritual Master.
   A Hermitage Ashram is a remote Ashram where the Spiritual Master retreats from the "busy-ness" of the world. The principal Hermitage Ashram of Heart-Master Da Love-Ananda is Sri Love-Anandashram in Fiji. The Mountain Of Attention in northern California and Tumomama in Hawaii are the two other Hermitage Ashrams where Heart-Master Da has lived.

5. Heart-Master Da [Love-Ananda], *Look at the Sunlight on the Water: Educating Children for a Life of self-Transcending Love and Happiness—An Introduction* (Clearlake, Calif.: The Dawn Horse Press, 1983), pp. 107-9, 80-81, 110.

6. Rato Khyongla Nawang Losang, *My Life and Lives: The Story of a Tibetan Incarnation* (New York: E. P. Dutton, 1977), p. 15.

7. Chogyam Trungpa, *Journey Without Goal: The Tantric Wisdom of the Buddha* (Boston and London: Shambhala, 1985), pp. 97-98.

8. Ibid., pp. 98-99.

9. In the Way of the Heart, the term "conscious exercise" has several meanings. First, it refers to the way practitioners radiate love with their whole being—with their heart-feeling and their breath, with their bodies, and by allowing their attention to be free in the moment. It also refers to the ways that Heart-Master Da Love-Ananda has Instructed His devotees to move bodily. He has Given us great practical Wisdom about the Happiest way to sit, stand, walk, and breathe. It also refers to the balancing and enlivening exercise routines that devotees do at the beginning and end of each day. To sum it up, conscious exercise is the practical discipline of living as love with your whole body.

10. In *What and Where and Who To Remember To Be Happy, A Simple Explanation Of The Way Of The Heart (For Children, and Everyone Else)*, Heart-Master Da Love-Ananda describes—in a very simple and direct way—how everyone can practice remembering and feeling and breathing and loving and Being the Mystery all the time. He also Gives very useful Instruction specifically for children about how to practice Remembering the Mystery, or Divine Happiness, in meditation. The meditation practice that He Gives in this book is engaged by all early-life practitioners in the Way of the Heart, from the time they are very small until they are about fourteen years old.

11. Heart-Master Da Love-Ananda has Revealed that the process of human development occurs in seven stages, and He has outlined the forms of practical and meditative discipline appropriate to each stage of life in the Way of the Heart (including those for children and young people). Because Heart-Master Da Himself has fulfilled the requirements of all these stages, and has Realized the seventh, or Divinely Self-Realized, stage of life, He offers Perfect and effective Wisdom to everyone who would live in the Feeling of the Divine Mystery.

The First Three Stages. These generally correspond to the first three periods of seven years as we grow from infancy to adulthood, and are a "school" where we learn to become truly human. Heart-Master Da's Instructions about the first three stages of life tell us exactly how to become responsible, creatively alive, and loving—physically, emotionally, and mentally. Because the responsibilities of maturing in the first three stages are great, most people spend even their adult lives still concentrated in one or another of these first three stages of development.

In the first stage of life, from the time you are conceived until you are about seven years old, you learn to be responsible for the "vital-physical" aspects of your existence—for holding things, walking, talking, feeding yourself, converting food and breath into energy, and learning how to relate to other people, such as your family and your close friends.

The second stage of life generally begins when you are mature in the first stage of life, when you are about seven years old (although signs of second stage development may appear earlier). In this stage you become aware of and responsible for what you are beyond your physical existence. You learn about the feeling, or "etheric", dimension, and you develop as a moral character, or someone who knows how to relate to others as love. You learn how to participate happily, as love and with real energy, in a larger sphere of social relations.

Growth in the third stage of life occurs from about the time when you are fourteen years old (although signs of third stage development may appear earlier) until you are approximately twenty-one. Heart-Master Da says regarding the third stage of life:

[The third stage of life] involves development of the will, the thinking mind, and the mind of the psyche. The individual should already have developed as a physical, feeling, and moral character, fully in touch with the Living Force of existence. Thus, in the third stage, this personality must develop the will to rightly and fruitfully use the Life-Force in the context of psyche, mind, body, and relations with others in the natural world. . . .

The third stage of life is complete when the individual is fully responsible for adult life—not merely in the conventional social sense, or merely because of chronological age, but in the sense that he or she is fully prepared (physically, emotionally, etherically, psychically, mentally, and with a free or intelligent will) to enter into the social, personal, and spiritual responsibilities of true Manhood. (Look at the Sunlight on the Water, pp. 33-34)

After the third stage of life, the last four stages of possible human growth do not correspond to periods of time, but to stages of Spiritual understanding that can be realized by adults of any age. But because a person must mature in each stage before he or she can fully participate in the next (and because, historically, most people do not complete the process of growth in the first three stages of life), very few move into the fourth stage of life or beyond. Those who have made the transition to the advanced and ultimate stages of life are the Saints, Yogis, Mystics, Adepts, and God-Realized Masters whose exceptional participation in the Sacred Process has inspired all the great religious and Spiritual traditions of humanity.

The Fourth Stage. Traditionally, the fourth stage of life is the stage of heart-felt surrender and profoundly absorbing intimacy with God, cultivated through prayer, meditation, self-discipline, and bodily service. The fourth stage Saints tend erroneously to perceive God as a Great "Other" (outside or apart from themselves) with Whom they must always strive to be reunited. In the Way of the Heart, fourth stage practitioners, through feeling-Contemplation of Heart-Master Da Love-Ananda, are drawn beyond the stress of this fourth stage tendency into present and immediate heart-intimacy with Heart-Master Da.

The Fifth Stage. Traditionally, practitioners in the fifth stage of life stimulate the visionary centers of the brain and nervous system through Yogic disciplines so that they can ascend beyond gross awareness to awareness of the subtle realms. Such fifth stage Yogis and Mystics feel they Commune with God most directly through these extraordinary and blissful experiences.

Fifth stage practitioners in the Way of the Heart may have these traditionally prized experiences also, but their practice is to continue to feel beyond whatever extraordinary experiences may arise, because, through their feeling-Contemplation of Heart-Master Da, they realize that no experience, no matter how blissful, contains the Happiness or Love-Bliss found as and in Heart-Master Da, Who Is Infinitely Awake before anything at all arises.

The Sixth Stage. Traditionally, practitioners in the sixth stage of life understand that their True Self is the Blissful Divine Mystery Itself, but they tend to feel that the body, the mind, and the world (or anything they can experience) are different from the True Self and the Happy Play of the Divine Mystery. In the Way of the Heart, sixth stage practitioners transcend everything, even this sense of difference, in Perfect Identification with Heart-Master Da as the One Person or Universal Self that is all Love-Bliss.

The Seventh Stage. In the seventh, or ultimate and final, stage of life, the devotee Realizes that there is Only the Mystery, Only Happiness, Only God, no matter what experience appears to arise, and even if nothing arises at all. Heart-Master Da calls this Divinely Enlightened Realization "Open Eyes", because such a devotee sees that everything arising is totally transparent to the "Bright" Divine

Mystery. Seventh stage devotees in the Way of the Heart continue to surrender to Heart-Master Da as the Giving Source of their unbroken Happiness.

In the Way of the Heart, the seventh stage Realization is that all that arises is the "One Feeling" that is the Mystery, or Love-Bliss. This Feeling is the Guide and the Inspiration for practice at every stage in the Way of the Heart.

The practice of meditation, which is always founded on feeling-Contemplation of the "Bright" Form of Heart-Master Da Love-Ananda, deepens in each of these progressive stages of life. And, as their stage of life matures, practitioners in the Way of the Heart take greater and greater responsibility for this foundation practice of feeling-Contemplation through technical forms of responsibility and practice that Heart-Master Da Love-Ananda has designated for each stage.

Heart-Master Da Love-Ananda has fully described the various forms of meditative practice He recommends for each stage of life and practice in His Sacred Teaching literature.

12. Heart-Master Da [Love-Ananda], *Look at the Sunlight on the Water*, pp. 109, 82, 110.

ABOUT THE WORLD-TEACHER, HEART-MASTER DA LOVE-ANANDA

1. The World-Teacher, Heart-Master Da Love-Ananda, *The Knee of Listening*, New Standard Edition. Forthcoming.

2. *The Knee of Listening.*

3. *The Knee of Listening.*

4. *The Knee of Listening.*

5. *The Knee of Listening.*

6. *I Am Happiness: A Rendering for Children of the Spiritual Adventure of Master Da Free John [Heart-Master Da Love-Ananda].* Adapted by Daji Bodha and Lynne Closser from *The Knee of Listening* by Heart-Master Da Love-Ananda. (Clearlake, Calif.: The Dawn Horse Press, 1982), p. 52.

7. Saniel Bonder, *The Divine Emergence of The World-Teacher: The Realization, the Revelation, and the Revealing Ordeal of Heart-Master Da Love-Ananda* (Clearlake, Calif.: The Dawn Horse Press, 1990), p. 336.

8. *The Dawn Horse Testament Of The World-Teacher, Heart-Master Da Love-Ananda,* New Standard Edition. Forthcoming.

CHAPTER 1

1. Heart-Master Da Love-Ananda has Taught us that to "consider" something is not just to talk about it or to think about it. To "consider" something in the Way of the Heart is to investigate it thoroughly—even by actively experimenting with whatever you are "considering"—until the truth of it becomes completely clear.

For instance, each practitioner in the Way of the Heart experiments with the forms of practice that Heart-Master Da Love-Ananda has Given us (within guidelines that He has provided). In this way, every practitioner "considers" and thereby discovers exactly how to use each practice to grow in Happiness.

2. The mala that the Brahmacharinis use in prayer and meditation is a garland of one hundred and eight beads (made of wood or seeds) plus one larger bead called the "Master bead", which is the Sign of Heart-Master Da. Devotees in the Way of the Heart may Contemplate Heart-Master Da by simply holding the mala or by touching each bead, one after the other, as they Invoke His Blessing by Remembering His Name, either silently or out loud. This cycle of prayer, which starts and ends with the Master bead, celebrates the devotional relationship to Heart-Master Da as if the devotee were moving around Him in a joyous circle of worship.

CHAPTER 2

1. Heart-Master Da Love-Ananda often Serves His devotees by Offering His observations about their practice. When Heart-Master Da Love-Ananda Gives us His Guidance in this manner, the Kanyadana Kumaris write down what He says, so that His Instructions can be passed on to devotees.

All practitioners in the Way of the Heart know that to receive these Notes from Heart-Master Da Love-Ananda is a great Blessing, for His Words always convey His Blessing-Help for our practice of Happiness.

CHAPTER 3

1. For all the years of His Teaching Work, Heart-Master Da Love-Ananda consented to look and act like His devotees in order to Serve us. He even dressed up in scary or humorous costumes and celebrated Halloween with us!

But since His Divine Emergence and the beginning of His Blessing Work in 1986, Heart-Master Da Love-Ananda Serves us in a very different way. He no longer looks or acts like we do. Instead, He Asks us to feel Him and Contemplate Him and become like Him. And we have noticed that when we Contemplate Him with feeling, we become unreasonably Happy—and we feel the Freedom and Truth and Love That He Is.

CHAPTER 5

1. Swami Prakashananda was the headmaster of a brahmacharya school for boys in India. He was also a principal Indian devotee of Swami Muktananda, one of Heart-Master Da's Spiritual Teachers. Heart-Master Da Love-Ananda saw Swami Prakashananda several times at Swami Muktananda's residence in Bombay in 1969. Swami Prakashananda radiated so much Happiness that it made Heart-Master Da Happy just to look at him.

CHAPTER 8

1. Heart-Master Da not only lives in and as the Divine Mystery, but He spontaneously Communicates, or Radiates, or, as He says here, Transmits, the Love-Bliss of the Mystery to others. People experience many effects of Heart-Master Da's

Transmission of Happiness, such as blissful energies in the body or visions. But Heart-Master Da's Transmission is much more Powerful and Liberating than these effects. His Transmission is a silent Communication of the Mystery of the Heart, or Happiness Itself, that can be felt no matter what the body-mind is experiencing—and even if no body or mind arises.

2. The foundation of all practice in the Way of the Heart (no matter what your age or stage of life) is feeling-Contemplation of Heart-Master Da Love-Ananda's bodily (human) Form, His Spiritual (and Always Blessing) Presence, and His Very (and Inherently Perfect) State.

Heart-Master Da's bodily (human) Form constantly and perfectly Radiates His Heart-Blessing to everyone who will open their hearts to see and feel who He really Is. His Spiritual (and Always Blessing) Presence is the Radiant Energy of Happiness Itself, which Heart-Master Da constantly showers on those who are sensitive and alive to Him Spiritually. His Very (and Inherently Perfect) State is the Silence and Stillness and Perfect Fullness of Divine Happiness or Consciousness Itself.

3. *The Love-Ananda Gita* is one of Heart-Master Da's sacred texts about Happiness. In it, He Teaches us how to be Happy, by Contemplating or Remembering, with feeling, His bodily (human) Form, His Spiritual (and Always Blessing) Presence, and His Very (and Inherently Perfect) State.

CHAPTER 9

1. Surya Namaskar (which means "salutation to the sun") is a Hatha Yoga exercise consisting of a series of poses designed to balance and enliven the body. As a Brahmacharini, Shawnee practiced "Da Namaskar" ("salutation to Da"), which is similar to the traditional Surya Namaskar, but which Heart-Master Da has transformed into a devotional exercise in the Way of the Heart. While she was under discipline, Brahmacharini Shawnee returned to the traditional form of Surya Namaskar.

2. The Giving Coat is a sacred hall at Sri Love-Anandashram Hermitage Ashram. It is alive with the Feeling of the Mystery because Sat-Guru Da Love-Ananda has spent many hours there in sacred occasions with devotees.

CHAPTER 10

1. "Love-Ananda" is one of Heart-Master Da's Names that is used formally by all devotees in the Way of the Heart, but always in conjunction with His other Titles and Names. Members of the Hridaya Da Gurukula (that is, the Kanyas and the four Brahmacharinis) are the only devotees of Heart-Master Da to use His Name "Love-Ananda" by itself when they speak to or about Heart-Master Da Love-Ananda.

2. A conch is a shell used in many sacred traditions, because when it is blown, the sound brings the feeling energy of the body to life. Whenever Heart-Master Da takes a walk—for instance, if He walks from His home in the village to the library of Sri Love-Anandashram—devotees blow a large conch to celebrate His appearance in the village and to call everyone to receive His Darshan. The sound of the conch in Sri Love-Anandashram is one of the sounds devotees most love to hear.

3. The Raising of the Giving Tree in early December begins the period of preparation for The Feast of the Love-Ananda Leela (formerly known as The Feast of God in Every Body). The Giving Tree, which symbolizes the body of every living being, is decorated with lights and colored ornaments to glorify and celebrate the Divine Life that is alive in and as everyone.

4. "Tcha" is the sacred sound that Heart-Master Da characteristically makes as a form of Blessing. You could say that it is a meaningless word because there is no definition for it in the dictionary. But if you hear Heart-Master Da say this word, your heart immediately knows the definition of "Tcha". Its meaning is Love.

5. "Asana" is a Sanskrit word meaning "sitting down", and it generally refers to the position of your body. But it also sometimes refers to the exercises of body and breath and feeling and even attention that you engage when practicing certain forms of Yoga. Heart-Master Da also uses "asana" in a larger sense, to mean your entire attitude or orientation in any given moment.

CHAPTER 11

1. Heart-Master Da Love-Ananda has observed and described three distinct character types, or ways that we tend to dramatize un-Happiness, which He calls "solid", "vital", and "peculiar".

Solid people tend to think a lot and try to control themselves and others. Solid types, in general, can be strong physically but they tend not to express themselves emotionally very well.

The vital personality is very enthusiastic about finding pleasure in the body—by eating, talking, and in general "doing" too much. When the vital person's outgoing and enthusiastic "up" phase is over, he or she tends to swing into a negative period of being tired and frustrated or feeling self-pity.

The peculiar type tends to be very emotional and given to flights of fantasy. Peculiars do not like to bring strength to their vital life, and as a result they are usually physically weak and somewhat withdrawn.

2. From 1966 until 1969, Heart-Master Da kept a diary about His life and Spiritual practice. This diary later became a book, which He called *Water and Narcissus*. Devotees who read the manuscript of *Water and Narcissus* (which is kept at the Hermitage Ashrams for this purpose) are inspired by the insights (into the errors we make as "Narcissus") and the wisdom (about standing Free of "Narcissus") that the book contains.

3. All practitioners of the Way of the Heart study Swami Muktananda's book *Ashram Dharma* to learn about the tradition of what one should and should not do in the Sat-Guru's Ashram. Swami Muktananda, a Spiritual Teacher who lived and Taught in India, was Heart-Master Da Love-Ananda's Teacher from 1968 to 1970. He helped Heart-Master Da by Teaching Him about the higher Yogic processes of the body-mind.

4. Swami Rudrananda (also known as Rudi) was Heart-Master Da's first human Teacher, from 1964 to 1968. Rudi's book *Spiritual Cannibalism* contains some of the instruction about the foundation stages of Spiritual life that he gave to Heart-Master Da. Rudi was a Master of the vital energies of the body-mind, and he helped Heart-Master Da to become strong in devotion, service, self-discipline, and meditation. Rudi passed Heart-Master Da on to his own Guru, Swami Muktananda, for instruction in the more mature phases of Spiritual practice.

5. The Sanskrit word "leela" (sometimes spelled "lila") means "play", or "sport". In the Spiritual traditions, everything that exists and everything that happens is seen to be the spontaneous and effortless Play, or "Leela", of the Divine Person. "Leela" also describes the Divinely Awakened and Always Blessing Play of the Sat-Guru. In the Way of the Heart, devotees refer to any of the Heart-Enlivening, Heart-Instructive, and Heart-Awakening Stories about Heart-Master Da's Teaching and Blessing Work, or Play, as a Leela.

6. Between and just slightly above your eyebrows and behind your forehead is a point of energy called the "ajna chakra", which is one of seven such chakras, or centers of energy, in your body. It is sometimes called the "third eye" or the "ajna door", because it is the place in the body where the Spiritual Blessing-Force of the Sat-Guru "enters" the devotee.

7. When Heart-Master Da was a little boy, He was especially fond of tapioca pudding for dessert. One day when He found a dish of tapioca pudding that His mother had made for Him, He was so excited and happy that He grabbed the dish of pudding and skipped and leaped and jumped all over the house, laughing with happiness. His mother heard Him laughing and came to see what had made Him so happy. He was laughing so hard that He tripped and fell. The dish of pudding flew out of His hand, and the tapioca pudding splattered against the ceiling and then dripped all over Heart-Master Da as He lay on the floor. Now it was His mother's turn to laugh at Him, and she and Heart-Master Da laughed so hard together with love and Happiness that tears ran down their faces.

8. *The Basket of Tolerance* is a book by Heart-Master Da Love-Ananda that contains a bibliography of all the most important sacred texts from all the great religious and Spiritual Teachings of humankind. Heart-Master Da has also written many essays in *The Basket of Tolerance* which describe how each of these traditions is speaking (in its own way) about one (or more) of the seven stages of life.

9. The "arati" is a traditional ceremony of waving lights around the Body of the Sat-Guru. Devotees do this (either around the physical Form of the Sat-Guru or around a representation of the Sat-Guru's physical Form, such as a photograph) to express their Happiness, devotion, and gratitude. At the Hermitage Ashrams of the Way of the Heart, devotees perform the Sat-Guru Arati at the closing of each day by chanting, waving lights and incense, and making ecstatic sounds with musical instruments.

10. "Siddha" is a Sanskrit word meaning "Completed One", or One Whose Happiness in God is Complete and Who is also perfectly Full of Blessing Power. Heart-Master Da is a Hridaya-Siddha, or One Who Transmits the "Bright" Divine Power of the Heart Itself (rather than the secondary powers of Yoga that some traditional Siddhas in the fourth and fifth stages of life transmit).

11. "Seva" is a Sanskrit word that means "service". Guru-Seva, or service to one's Guru, is an ancient practice that has been honored as a very important aspect of Spiritual practice in many traditions. In the Way of the Heart, Sat-Guru-Seva is a truly Happy practice because by serving Heart-Master Da, we forget our un-Happiness and remember His joyous Heart-Blessing instead.

12. The Feast of God in Every Body, which practitioners in the Way of the Heart now call The Feast of the Love-Ananda Leela, is the Spiritual celebration that we observe each year at the time also associated with Christmas. It is a time when we celebrate all the many Gifts of Blessing that Heart-Master Da Love-Ananda has Given His devotees. We do this especially by celebrating the Gift of our community, giving gifts to Heart-Master Da Love-Ananda and to one another, and by telling one another the Stories of His Giving Work.

13. Because The Matrix is the place where Heart-Master Da maintains His primary and most private Residence, it is one of the most sacred places at Sri Love-Anandashram. It is a place of great Beauty, Radiance, and Heart-Happiness, and devotees honor it as the place where their Divine Heart-Master Lives in Freedom.

14. All living things must take in what they need to live and eliminate what they do not need and cannot use. Heart-Master Da calls this cycle "reception-release". One very basic way we participate in the cycle of reception-release is through the breath, and Heart-Master Da recommends that children (as well as adults) consciously remember to "breathe in the good stuff" and "breathe out the bad stuff".

CHAPTER 12

1. The World-Teacher, Heart-Master Da Love-Ananda, *What and Where and Who To Remember To Be Happy*, New Standard Edition. Forthcoming.

2. The years of Heart-Master Da's Work to awaken others have been marked by many auspicious times when He Demonstrated His Great Blessing Power in most obvious, even Miraculous, and always Compassionate ways. The Love of the God-Man Celebration, which was held in March of 1984 at The Mountain Of Attention Hermitage Ashram, was such a time. Over a ten-day period, devotees gathered frequently with Heart-Master Da while He Granted His Blessing-Darshan. On those occasions they celebrated their love for Him with great joy through chant, song, recitation of sacred texts, meditation, and other forms of worship and praise.

3. The Way of the Heart is made of Seven Gifts of Grace, all of which Heart-Master Da Freely Gives to all His devotees, at every stage of life.

The Seven Gifts of the Hridaya-Samartha Sat-Guru's Grace are: (1) Word, or Heart-Master Da's Teaching of Happiness and all the Inspiring and Instructive Stories about Him; (2) Sign, or Heart-Master Da's bodily (human) Form, His Spiritual (and Always Blessing) Presence, and His Very (and Inherently Perfect) State, which are Radiant Happiness in Person; (3) Devotion, or heart-response to His Perfect Happiness; (4) Service, or the practice of expressing Happiness by giving energy to Heart-Master Da, your family, your friends, and everyone; (5) Discipline, or all the many practical means that Heart-Master Da Gives His devotees to Remember Him (including exercise, right diet, and personal disciplines that discipline the body—in addition to study of His Teaching and His Leelas and forms of prayer, meditation, and worship that discipline attention); (6) Blessing, or the Happy Feeling that you can feel whenever you remember to feel and breathe and Behold and even Be the Mystery that is Heart-Master Da; and (7) Blessedness, or the Freedom to feel and Be Happiness, or the Mystery Itself, which can only be Realized on the basis of the other six Gifts, in Heart-Communion with Heart-Master Da.

CHAPTER 13

1. When a Jewish girl reaches the age of thirteen, she is welcomed into the responsibilities of the adult culture by her relatives and friends in a ceremony called "bas mitzvah". (The similar ceremony for boys is called "bar mitzvah".)

CHAPTER 15

1. "Satsang" is an ancient Hindu term that means "Good Company". In the Hindu tradition (as in all other religious and Spiritual traditions) it is understood that the very best thing anyone can do is to spend time in the Company of those who have Realized Divine Happiness. In the Way of the Heart, we use the term "Satsang" to refer to the sacred relationship devotees enjoy with Heart-Master Da Love-Ananda whenever they Contemplate Him with feeling and receive His Blessings by practicing exactly as He has described. Thus, Satsang is the mutual relationship between Heart-Master Da Love-Ananda and His devotee.

CHAPTER 16

1. Heart-Master Da [Love-Ananda], *Look at the Sunlight on the Water*, back cover.

2. *Look at the Sunlight on the Water*, pp. 76, 78.

CHAPTER 19

1. In the Hindu tradition and in the Way of the Heart, "Prasad" is a word used to describe anything that the Sat-Guru Blesses and gives to devotees. In Darshan occasions at Sri Love-Anandashram, Heart-Master Da Love-Ananda most often Blesses small sweets, which are then distributed to devotees at the closing of the occasion as a special form of His Blessing.

Further Notes to the Reader

(Continued from copyright page)

An Invitation to Responsibility

The Way of the Heart that Heart-Master Da Love-Ananda has Revealed is an invitation to everyone to assume real responsibility for his or her life. As Heart-Master Da has Said in *The Dawn Horse Testament*, "If any one Is Interested In The Realization Of The Heart, Let him or her First Submit (By Heart) To Me, and (Thereby) Commence The Ordeal Of self-Observation, self-Understanding, and self-Transcendence." Therefore, participation in the Way of the Heart requires a real struggle with oneself, and not at all a struggle with Heart-Master Da, or with others.

All who study the Way of the Heart or take up its practice should remember that they are responding to a Call to become responsible for themselves. They should understand that they, not Heart-Master Da or others, are responsible for any decision they may make or action they may take in the course of their lives of study or practice. This has always been true, and it is true whatever the individual's involvement in the Way of the Heart, be it as one who studies Heart-Master Da's Wisdom-Teaching, or as a formal "Friend" of The Free Daist Communion, or as a formally acknowledged practitioner of the Way of the Heart.

Honoring and Protecting the Sacred Word through Perpetual Copyright

Since ancient times, practitioners of true religion and Spirituality have valued, above all, time spent in the Company of the Sat-Guru, or One Who has Realized God, Truth, or Reality, and Who Serves that same Realization in others. Such practitioners understand that the Sat-Guru literally Transmits His or Her (Realized) State to every one (and every thing) with which He or She comes in contact. Through this Transmission, objects, environments, and rightly prepared individuals with which the Sat-Guru has contact can become Empowered, or Imbued with the Sat-Guru's Transforming Power. It is by this process of Empowerment that things and beings are made truly and literally sacred, and things so sanctified thereafter function as a Source of the Sat-Guru's Blessing for all who understand how to make right and sacred use of them.

The Sat-Guru and all that He Empowers are, therefore, truly Sacred Treasures, for they help draw the practitioner more quickly into the Realization of Perfect Identity with the Divine Self. Cultures of true Wisdom have always understood that such Sacred Treasures are precious (and fragile) Gifts to humanity, and that they should be honored, protected, and reserved for right sacred use. Indeed, the word "sacred" means "set apart", and thus protected, from the secular world. Heart-Master Da Love-Ananda is a Sat-Guru of the Perfect degree. He has Conformed His body-mind completely to the Divine Self, and He is thus a most Potent Source of Blessing-Transmission of God, Truth, or Reality. He has for many years Empowered, or made sacred, special places and things, and these now Serve as His Divine Agency, or as literal expressions and extensions of His Blessing-Transmission. Among these Empowered Sacred Treasures is His Wisdom-Teaching, which is Full of His Transforming Power. This Blessed and Blessing Wisdom-Teaching has Mantric Force, or the literal Power to Serve God-Realization in those who are Graced to receive it.

Therefore, Heart-Master Da Love-Ananda's Teaching Word must be perpetually honored and protected, "set apart" from all possible interference and wrong use. The Free Daist Communion, which is the fellowship of devotees of Heart-Master Da Love-Ananda, is committed to the perpetual preservation and right honoring of the sacred Wisdom-Teaching of the Way of the Heart. But it is also true that in order to fully accomplish this, we must find support in the world-society in which we live and from the laws under which we live. Thus, we call for a world-society and for laws that acknowledge the Sacred, and that permanently protect It from insensitive, secular interference and wrong use of any kind. We call for, among other things, a system of law that acknowledges that the Wisdom-Teaching of the Way of the Heart, in all Its forms, is, because of Its sacred nature, protected by perpetual copyright.

We invite others who respect the Sacred to join with us in this call and in working toward its realization. And, even in the meantime, we claim perpetual copyright to the Wisdom-Teaching of Heart-Master Da Love-Ananda and the other sacred literature and recordings of the Way of the Heart.

Heart-Master Da Love-Ananda and His Spiritual Instruments and Agents

Heart-Master Da Love-Ananda Speaks and Writes of His Spiritually, Transcendentally, and Divinely Awakened renunciate devotees as Agents or Instruments strictly in the Spiritual, Transcendental, and Divine sense, rather than in any worldly sense. He uses the word "Instrumentality" to indicate the formally acknowledged function of His Spiritually maturing or mature renunciate devotees to magnify (and, thus, naturally, and in a devotional manner, to serve) the Transmission of His Spiritual Blessing (and, possibly, His Transcendental and Ultimate Divine Revelation) to practitioners in their own stage of life or in earlier stages of life in the Way of the Heart.

Heart-Master Da uses the word "Agency" to indicate the formally Acknowledged and Empowered Capability and Function of specially chosen Divinely Self-Realized free renunciate devotees to directly Transmit His Spiritual, Transcendental, and Divine Heart-Blessing to all other practitioners of the Way of the Heart.

The first Means of Agency and Instrumentality that have been fully established by Heart-Master Da are the Wisdom-Teaching of the Way of the Heart and the three Hermitage Ashrams, or Sanctuaries, that He has Empowered. Human Agents and human Instruments are so acknowledged by Heart-Master Da or, after (and forever after) the physical Lifetime of His bodily (human) Form, by His specially appointed renunciate devotees (who, optimally, are His then presently living, and previously formally acknowledged, human Agents). And all such human Agents and human Instruments are thus acknowledged only (and more and more) as practitioners grow in the practice of the Way of the Heart and show signs of the specific capability to fulfill the formal responsibilities of either Agency or Instrumentality for Heart-Master Da's Blessing-Transmission within the formal cultural context of The Free Daist Communion.

Heart-Master Da Love-Ananda
Is a True Renunciate

Heart-Master Da Love-Ananda is a legal renunciate of The Free Daist Communion. Therefore, the Communion provides a living circumstance for Him and is authorized to publish His Talks and Writings. Heart-Master Da Functions only sacredly, and in Freedom. For many years He has owned nothing and has had no worldly responsibilities and has exercised no worldly functions. He has been and is a true renunciate. Heart-Master Da does not direct, and has not directed in any way, any of the activities of the Communion or of its representatives or members. Nor is Heart-Master Da responsible for any of the activities of The Free Daist Communion, its representatives, or its members.

The Guru-devotee Relationship
in the Way of the Heart

The Free Daist Communion does not guarantee its members, friends, and associates either a personal audience with Heart-Master Da or any specific experiences or Initiations. The process of Transmission is a living process of cultivating the relationship to Heart-Master Da as Sat-Guru, and that process follows its own laws. Neither Sat-Guru Da nor the Spiritual, Transcendental, and Divine Process can be strictly "institutionalized". The experiences or Realizations that may arise in the course of practice of the Way of the Heart depend on many factors—including, very fundamentally, each individual's genuine participation, readiness, right disposition, and personally auspicious characteristics. Heart-Master Da Freely and constantly Gives His Heart-Blessing to all, and It is received by each one according to his or her capability.

Publications

The Written and Spoken Teaching Word of The World-Teacher, Heart-Master Da Love-Ananda

My opinion is that we have, in the person of Heart-Master Da, a Spiritual Master and religious genius of the ultimate degree. [His] teaching is, I believe, unsurpassed by that of any other spiritual teacher, of any period, of any place, of any time, of any persuasion.

—Ken Wilber, author, *The Spectrum of Consciousness; Up from Eden*

Only One Who has Realized the Truth is Free to speak and live the Truth to others. The World-Teacher, Heart-Master Da Love-Ananda, speaks and writes with full Consciousness of the Infinite Life of the Heart. When such a Free Voice speaks, then the Power of the Word has become the Divine Agent for the Awakening and Liberation of others. The Teaching Word of Sat-Guru Da belongs to the ancient class of literature respectfully known as "sruti", or Teachings Revealed directly by the Divine Person, through the Divinely Self-Realized Sat-Guru. Therefore, to read or listen to Sat-Guru Da's Teaching Word is to feel (and thereby Contemplate) the Divine Being, Truth, Reality, or Happiness.

THE SOURCE LITERATURE

THE LOVE-ANANDA GITA
(THE WISDOM-SONG OF NON-SEPARATENESS)
The "Simple" Revelation-Book Of Da Kalki
(The World-Teacher, Heart-Master Da Love-Ananda)

Heart-Master Da's quintessential Revelation of the Way of the Heart. Because *The Love-Ananda Gita* contains His purest and simplest Call to Satsang, or feeling-Contemplation of His bodily (human) Form, His Spiritual (and Always Blessing) Presence, and His Very (and Inherently Perfect) State, it is the most basic Source Text of Heart-Master Da's entire Teaching Word.
Standard Edition
$34.95 cloth, $17.95 paper

THE DA ASHVAMEDHA GITA
(THE WISDOM-SONG OF DA KALKI
THE MASTER OF THE HORSE-SACRIFICE)
The Heart Of The "Dawn Horse" Revelations Of Da Kalki
(The World-Teacher, Heart-Master Da Love-Ananda)

This ecstatic epitome of Heart-Master Da Love-Ananda's Teaching-Revelation in *The Dawn Horse Testament* gives the general reader the essence of His Teaching Message in that mighty Source Text. *The Da Ashvamedha Gita* is the heart of Heart-Master Da's "Eternal Conversation" with everyone, His summary Teaching Word on the venerable Love-Yoga of Communion with Him as the Hridaya-Samartha Sat-Guru and, thus and thereby, with the Divine Person.
Standard Edition (forthcoming, late 1990)
$45.00 cloth, $19.95 paper

THE DAWN HORSE TESTAMENT
THE "TESTAMENT OF SECRETS" OF DA KALKI
(THE WORLD-TEACHER, HEART-MASTER DA LOVE-ANANDA)

Heart-Master Da's Ecstatic summary of the Way of the Heart, which He has progressively Revealed from 1970 until the present. In this monumental text of over 1,200 pages, Heart-Master Da Reveals the Mysteries and devotional Secrets of every form and developmental stage of the Way of the Heart He Offers to all who are prepared to practice it.
New Standard Edition (forthcoming, mid-1990)
$65.00 cloth, $75.00 cloth edition with slipcase, $29.95 paper

THE LION SUTRA
(ON PERFECT TRANSCENDENCE OF THE PRIMAL ACT,
WHICH IS THE ego-"I", THE self-CONTRACTION, OR attention itself,
AND ALL THE ILLUSIONS OF SEPARATION, OTHERNESS,
RELATEDNESS, AND "DIFFERENCE")
The "Radical" Revelation-Book Of Da Kalki
(The World-Teacher, Heart-Master Da Love-Ananda)

A fierce and beautiful poetic Exposition of the "radical", ultimate, and Inherently Perfect Practice of the Way of the Heart, particularly the final stages that lead to and include Transcendental, inherently Spiritual, and Divine Self-Realization. (An extensive revision of Heart-Master Da's Work formerly titled *Love-Ananda Gita*.)
New Standard Edition (forthcoming, early 1991)
$35.00 cloth, $17.95 paper

THE DA UPANISHAD
THE SHORT DISCOURSES ON self-RENUNCIATION,
GOD-REALIZATION, AND THE ILLUSION OF RELATEDNESS

Heart-Master Da's most concise Instruction relative to the forms of the Way of the Heart described in *The Dawn Horse Testament,* emphasizing the non-strategic, non-ascetical practice of renunciation in the Way of the Heart. (An extensive revision of Heart-Master Da's Work formerly titled *The Illusion Of Relatedness*.)
New Standard Edition
$49.95 cloth, $17.95 paper

THE BASKET OF TOLERANCE
A GUIDE TO PERFECT UNDERSTANDING OF THE ONE AND
GREAT TRADITION OF MANKIND

Heart-Master Da's Enlightened and discriminating evaluation of all the world's historical traditions of truly human culture, practical self-discipline, perennial religion, universal religious mysticism, "esoteric" (but now openly communicated) Spirituality, Transcendental Wisdom, and Perfect (or Divine) Enlightenment, compiled, annotated, and presented (with a comprehensive bibliography) by Heart-Master Da. The summary text of Heart-Master Da's Teaching Word on the Great Tradition of human Wisdom and the Sacred (Spiritual) Ordeal.
Standard Edition (forthcoming, late 1990)
$55.00 cloth, $22.95 paper

THE HYMN OF THE TRUE HEART-MASTER

(THE NEW REVELATION-BOOK OF THE ANCIENT AND
ETERNAL RELIGION OF DEVOTION TO THE GOD-REALIZED ADEPT)
FREELY EVOLVED FROM THE PRINCIPAL VERSES OF THE
TRADITIONAL *GURU GITA*

Heart-Master Da's new (seventh stage) version of the *Guru Gita* captures and surpasses the elegance of this ancient Sanskrit text and Reveals, with great poetic force and the authority of the Divine Self-Realizer, the Secrets of how to cultivate the relationship to Him as True Heart-Master.

New Standard Edition (forthcoming, early 1991)

$29.95 cloth, $14.95 paper

THE LIBERATOR (ELEUTHERIOS)

AN EPITOME OF PERFECT WISDOM AND "THE PERFECT PRACTICE"

In compelling poetic prose, Heart-Master Da distills the essence of Divine Self-Realization—the three stages of the ultimate process or "Perfect Practice" of direct transcendence of all experience in Consciousness Itself. Although what is described here is Heart-Master Da's ultimate prescription for practice, such is the potency of His Argument and Revelation that readers may find themselves able to intuit, if only momentarily, the ineffable Grace of Liberation.

New Standard Edition (forthcoming, early 1991)

$12.95 paper

INTRODUCTORY TEXTS

FREE DAISM

THE ETERNAL, ANCIENT, AND NEW RELIGION
OF GOD-REALIZATION

About the Divine alternative to the common life, an alternative traditionally Taught by Adept-Teachers in all ages, and which is now uniquely and most potently Offered in our own time by Heart-Master Da. Focusing on the basic elements of His popular Message, *Free Daism* introduces Heart-Master Da's "radical" and extremely practical Teaching Arguments, His Teaching and Blessing Work, and exactly what practice of the Way of the Heart, or "Free Daism", involves. Full of inspiring and insightful accounts by devotees, both new and old, who practice Free Daism today.

(forthcoming, mid-1990)

$12.95 paper

LOVE OF THE GOD-MAN
by James Steinberg

An extensive discussion of the absolute necessity of the Guru for those who desire to Realize God, Truth, Happiness, and Love, the profound laws and virtues of the Guru-devotee relationship as it has been practiced in many esoteric sacred traditions around the world, and the critical necessity to understand and transcend the sophistry of modern "anti-Guruism".

(forthcoming, mid-1990)

$14.95 paper

THE PRACTICAL TEXTS

THE EATING GORILLA COMES IN PEACE
THE TRANSCENDENTAL PRINCIPLE OF LIFE APPLIED TO DIET AND THE REGENERATIVE DISCIPLINE OF TRUE HEALTH

A manual of practical Wisdom about dietary practice, bodily health and well-being, and the sacred conduct of bodily life through all the stages of life and in death.

New Standard Edition (forthcoming, early 1991)

$19.95 paper

CONSCIOUS EXERCISE AND THE TRANSCENDENTAL SUN
THE PRINCIPLE OF LOVE APPLIED TO EXERCISE AND THE METHOD OF COMMON PHYSICAL ACTION (A SCIENCE OF WHOLE BODY WISDOM, OR TRUE EMOTION, INTENDED MOST ESPECIALLY FOR THOSE ENGAGED IN RELIGIOUS OR SPIRITUAL LIFE)

A practical guide to the practice of breath, exercise, and the science of whole body happiness.

New Standard Edition (forthcoming, early 1991)

$17.95 paper

LOVE OF THE TWO-ARMED FORM
THE FREE AND REGENERATIVE FUNCTION OF SEXUALITY IN
ORDINARY LIFE, AND THE TRANSCENDENCE OF SEXUALITY
IN TRUE RELIGIOUS OR SPIRITUAL PRACTICE

The original Teaching Word of Heart-Master Da Love-Ananda on the
right practice of intimacy and truly human sexuality.
New Standard Edition (forthcoming, mid-1991)
$19.95 paper

EASY DEATH
TALKS AND ESSAYS ON THE INHERENT AND
ULTIMATE TRANSCENDENCE OF DEATH
AND EVERYTHING ELSE

Heart-Master Da's authoritative Revelation of the process of death,
including His Compassionate Instructions on how to prepare for and
pass through it.
New Standard Edition (forthcoming, early 1991)
$17.95 paper

THE WISDOM LITERATURE OF HEART-MASTER DA LOVE-ANANDA'S TEACHING WORK

Heart-Master Da Love-Ananda's passionate commitment to the
Liberation of all beings lives in the essays and discourses within the
books listed in this section. They are the unique record of His constant
"Consideration" and Confession of Divine Enlightenment during the years
of His active Teaching Work, and they also record His Teaching Word on
the Great Process of Satsang that He Gracefully Offers to all.

Available in revised Standard Editions, the original texts of these
unsurpassed Scriptures of Heart-Master Da's Teaching-Revelation are now
accompanied by completely new introductory and other explanatory
material that contextualizes each book within Heart-Master Da's total
Teaching Work, which was fulfilled in His Divine Emergence in 1986.
Each book includes the leela, or story, of the Teaching Demonstration
that produced the Teaching Word summarized in the book, and explains
its relationship to His current and ongoing Blessing Work as summarized
most specifically in the eight Source Texts of His Teaching Word.

THE KNEE OF LISTENING
(THE LIFE-ORDEAL AND THE "RADICAL" SPIRITUAL
UNDERSTANDING OF "FRANKLIN JONES")

A unique record of the Spiritual, Transcendental, and Divine Ordeal and "radical" Enlightenment of Heart-Master Da, with His early essays on the practice and Realization of "Radical" Understanding. This original, unabridged manuscript, together with current commentary by Heart-Master Da and devotees, is nearly twice the length of the previously published edition. Foreword by Alan Watts.
New Standard Edition (forthcoming, mid-1991)
$14.95 paper

THE METHOD OF THE SIDDHAS
TALKS WITH "FRANKLIN JONES" [DA KALKI]
ON THE SPIRITUAL TECHNIQUE
OF THE SAVIORS OF MANKIND

In this book of talks with students in 1972 and 1973, the first year of His formal Teaching Work, Heart-Master Da Reveals the secret of the Way of Satsang that He Offers—the profound and transforming relationship between the Sat-Guru and His devotee.
New Standard Edition (forthcoming, mid-1991)
$14.95 paper

SCIENTIFIC PROOF OF THE EXISTENCE OF GOD WILL SOON BE ANNOUNCED BY THE WHITE HOUSE!
(PROPHETIC WISDOM ABOUT THE MYTHS AND IDOLS OF
MASS CULTURE AND POPULAR RELIGIOUS CULTISM, THE NEW
PRIESTHOOD OF SCIENTIFIC AND POLITICAL MATERIALISM, AND
THE SECRETS OF ENLIGHTENMENT HIDDEN IN THE BODY OF MAN)

Speaking as a modern Prophet, Heart-Master Da combines His urgent critique of present-day society with a challenge to create true sacred community based on actual Divine Communion and a Spiritual and "radically" Transcendental Vision of human Destiny.
New Standard Edition (forthcoming, late 1991)
$19.95 paper

THE TRANSMISSION OF DOUBT
TALKS AND ESSAYS ON THE TRANSCENDENCE
OF SCIENTIFIC MATERIALISM THROUGH
"RADICAL" UNDERSTANDING

Heart-Master Da's principal critique of scientific materialism, the dominant philosophy and world-view of modern humanity that suppresses our native impulse to Liberation, and His Revelation of the ancient and ever-new Way that is the true sacred science of Life, or of Divine Being Itself.

New Standard Edition (forthcoming, late 1991)
$17.95 paper

THE ENLIGHTENMENT OF THE WHOLE BODY
(A RATIONAL AND NEW PROPHETIC REVELATION
OF THE TRUTH OF RELIGION, ESOTERIC SPIRITUALITY,
AND THE DIVINE DESTINY OF MAN)

One of Heart-Master Da's early Revelations of the Way of Eternal Life that He Offers to beings everywhere, including praise of the All-Pervading Life and Transcendental Divine Consciousness, ecstatic Confessions of His Own Enlightened Condition, and sublime Instruction in each of the practices of the Way of the Heart. When initially published in 1978, this text represented the culmination of Heart-Master Da's Communication of the totality of His Way of the Heart.

New Standard Edition (forthcoming, late 1991)
$24.95 paper

NIRVANASARA
"RADICAL" TRANSCENDENTALISM AND
THE INTRODUCTION OF ADVAITAYANA BUDDHISM

From the vantage point of His Identification with Divine Consciousness, Heart-Master Da critically appraises the sacred Wisdom-Culture of mankind, particularly focusing on the two most profound traditional esoteric formulations of sacred life and practice—Buddhism and Hindu nondualism (Advaita Vedanta). Here, Heart-Master Da announces and expounds upon His own Way of "Radical" Transcendentalism as the "Fourth Vehicle" of Buddhism—Advaitayana Buddhism, which is the continuation and fulfillment of the most profound esoteric Teachings of Buddhism and Hinduism.

New Standard Edition (forthcoming, late 1991)
$14.95 paper

THE SONG OF THE SELF SUPREME
(ASHTAVAKRA GITA)

Heart-Master Da's illuminating Preface to the *Ashtavakra Gita* is a unique commentary on this grand classic of Advaita Vedanta, which He calls a "free communication by an Enlightened or God-Realized Adept". As a Living and Divinely Enlightened (seventh stage) Adept, or Sat-Guru, Heart-Master Da is singularly qualified to Speak with Authority about the non-dualistic Truth that Ashtavakra extols with such iconoclastic fervor. In His extended Preface, Heart-Master Da discusses the *Ashtavakra Gita* in the context of the total Great Tradition of Spiritual and Transcendental Wisdom, and He identifies and discusses the characteristics of those rare texts and traditions that fully Communicate the Realization and "Point of View" of the seventh stage of life.
New Standard Edition (forthcoming, mid-1991)
$14.95 paper

ECSTATIC FICTION AND POETRY OF GOD-REALIZATION

THE MUMMERY

The Mummery is Heart-Master Da Love-Ananda's "Liturgical Drama" of mythical and archetypal Divine Revelation. Written in a few brief weeks in late 1969, but based on a unique "writing yoga" engaged over several years in the early 1960s, *The Mummery* spontaneously expresses the entire esotericism of His Realization and His Teaching Word in the paradoxical story of Raymond Darling. Raymond Darling grows beyond childhood, and life at home with Mom and Dad, into—and beyond—the mysteries of life and death in his impassioned love of the beautiful Quandra. Destined to be recognized as an unsurpassed work of esoteric fiction, *The Mummery* is simultaneously an autobiography and a prophecy of Heart-Master Da Love-Ananda's entire Life and Work, and, as He Himself discloses, "a cipher . . . a magical text whose meanings can never be exhausted". Accompanied by stunning full color illustrations.
(forthcoming, mid-1991)
$45.00 cloth, $19.95 paper

CRAZY DA MUST SING, INCLINED TO HIS WEAKER SIDE
CONFESSIONAL POEMS OF LIBERATION AND LOVE

Composed principally in the early 1970s and expressed spontaneously with the ardor of continuous, Divinely Awakened Identification with all beings, these remarkable poems proclaim Heart-Master Da Love-Ananda's vulnerable human Love and His mysterious, "Crazy" passion to Liberate others from ego-bondage.
New Standard Edition (forthcoming, mid-1991)
$12.95 paper

LEELAS

The Sanskrit term "leela" (sometimes "lila") traditionally refers to the Divine Play of the Sat-Guru with His devotees, whereby He Instructs and Liberates the world.

The leelas told by practitioners of the Way of the Heart document the years of Heart-Master Da Love-Ananda's active identification with and Submission to devotees as Adept Heart-Teacher, and His Work since His Divine Emergence in 1986. Heart-Master Da has said that Leelas of His Instructional Play with devotees are part of His own Teaching Word, and they are, therefore, Potent with the Blessing and Awakening-Power of His Heart-Transmission.

THE DIVINE EMERGENCE OF THE WORLD-TEACHER
THE REALIZATION, THE REVELATION, AND THE REVEALING ORDEAL OF DA KALKI
A Biographical Celebration of Heart-Master Da Love-Ananda
by Saniel Bonder

Never before have the Life and Mission of a seventh stage Divine Incarnation been so carefully documented. This lively narrative begins with Heart-Master Da Love-Ananda's Enlightened Birth, His "forgetting" of the "Bright" Divine State, and His arduous Ordeal of Re-Awakening, and it clarifies the benign nature of His "Crazy" Teaching Work with His early, Western devotees. The book's esoteric focus is Heart-Master Da's lifelong Ordeal of Divine Transmutation—which finally culminated, on January 11, 1986, in the Great Event that inaugurated His Divine

Emergence as The World-Teacher and His Universal Blessing Work that continues today.

Richly illustrated with more than 100 photographs of Heart-Master Da Love-Ananda, and full of the inspiring and often riveting Stories of His Teaching and Blessing Work as told by His devotees, as well as His own unique Confessions of Divine Incarnation, Realization, and Service to all beings.

$14.95 paper

THE CALLING OF THE KANYAS
CONFESSIONS OF SPIRITUAL AWAKENING AND "PERFECT PRACTICE" THROUGH THE LIBERATING GRACE OF DA KALKI (THE WORLD-TEACHER, HEART-MASTER DA LOVE-ANANDA)
by Meg Krenz with The Hridaya Da Gurukula Kanyadana Kumari Mandala (Kanya Tripura Rahasya, Kanya Remembrance, Kanya Kaivalya Navaneeta, and Kanya Suprithi)

This is the remarkable account of the Graceful ordeal of sacred practice and transformation embraced by the formal renunciate order of four women devotees who personally serve Sat-Guru Da Love-Ananda. *The Calling of the Kanyas* stands among the great devotional testimonies of illumined Saints and Seers in the sacred traditions. The confessions and the example of the Kanyas are a Calling to everyone to deeply understand and heartily respond to the Supremely Graceful Event that has made their own Spiritual transformation possible: Heart-Master Da's Great Divine Emergence in early 1986.

(forthcoming, early 1991)

$17.95 paper

LOSING FACE
by Frans Bakker, M.D.

A successful Dutch physician, Frans Bakker began to suspect a fundamental fault in the assumptions underlying not only his medical practice but his life itself. Here he tells stories from his years as a devotee of Heart-Master Da Love-Ananda. This account of the joyous and difficult ordeal of self-understanding he has embraced during Heart-Master Da's Teaching and Blessing Work will be of special interest to readers from a Western background who want to learn more about Heart-Master Da's Work and His popular Message.

(forthcoming, mid-1991)

$14.95 paper

DAU LOLOMA NAITAUBA
HOW DAU LOLOMA (DA KALKI) GAVE MANY HOLY BLESSINGS
TO THE PEOPLE OF FIJI AND MADE HIS ETERNAL SPIRITUAL HOME
ON THE ISLAND OF NAITAUBA
by Morton Whiteside

In 1983, Heart-Master Da Love-Ananda arrived on the island of
Naitauba, in Fiji, to establish it as His principal World-Teacher Ashram.
This extraordinary collection of leelas chronicles the Spiritually dramatic
events of Heart-Master Da's Enlightened interplay with the people of Fiji
and the spirit-forces He has encountered there.
(forthcoming, mid-1991)
$9.95 paper

THE LION MURTI OF DA KALKI
(THE WORLD-TEACHER,
HEART-MASTER DA LOVE-ANANDA)
by Kanya Kaivalya Navaneeta, Charles Seage, M.D.,
and Dan Bouwmeester, M.D.

Divine Enlightenment is evidenced by extraordinary Signs in the
body-mind. The authors of this remarkable document have carefully
recorded all the changes and unique Signs registered in Heart-Master Da
Love-Ananda's Transfigured body during the years of His Teaching and
Blessing Work to date. Heart-Master Da Himself has spoken extensively
about these processes and Signs, elucidating them for those interested in
the technical esoteric processes whereby He has Perfectly Incarnated the
Divine Self in and as His bodily (human) Form.
(forthcoming, early 1991)
$12.95 paper

TCHA
A compilation of many Leelas of Heart-Master Da Love-Ananda's
Teaching Work and Heart-Blessing of children and adults, men and
women—and animals as well—throughout the years of His Sacred Mission to date. Full of both miracles and the stories of hard-learned sacred
lessons, *Tcha* gives a vivid picture of a Divine Teacher and True Heart-
Master Whose every Gesture and Communication Imparts the Wisdom
and Happiness of Divine Freedom to others.
(forthcoming, mid-1991)
$14.95 paper

THE HORSE SACRIFICE
by Saniel Bonder

This book tells a story until now known in its fullness only by those who participated in it. It is a full-length Sacred History of Heart-Master Da's Life and His impassioned Struggle with devotees in the nearly two decades of His Mission as Adept Heart-Teacher and Hridaya-Samartha Sat-Guru. This unique record chronicles in extensive, vivid detail all the epochs of Heart-Master Da's Divinely Enlightened Life-Work that could only be briefly summarized in *The Divine Emergence of The World-Teacher*. A feast of the dramatic, Spirit-filled Leela of the God-Man of our epoch.

(forthcoming, late 1991)
$17.95 paper

DA NATARAJA

In His Indoor Yajna period of Teaching—His "last gesture" as a Teacher—from April 1987 through March 1988, Heart-Master Da Love-Ananda Taught not only by Word but by Dance. This unique collection of leelas records the extraordinary psychic and Spiritual Impact of the Dancing of One Who embodies the Heart-Spirit of the Dance as Divine Sacrifice in Love.

(forthcoming, late 1991)
$14.95 paper

FOR AND ABOUT CHILDREN

WHAT AND WHERE AND WHO
TO REMEMBER TO BE HAPPY
A SIMPLE EXPLANATION OF THE WAY OF
THE HEART (FOR CHILDREN, AND EVERYONE ELSE)

A new edition of Heart-Master Da's essential Teaching-Revelation on the religious principles and practices appropriate for children. In a "consideration" easily understood and enjoyed by children of all ages, Heart-Master Da tells children (and adults) how to "feel and breathe and Behold and Be the Mystery".

New Standard Edition, fully illustrated (forthcoming, early 1991)
$12.95 cloth, $8.95 paper

THE TWO SECRETS (yours, AND MINE)
A STORY OF HOW THE WORLD-TEACHER, DA KALKI,
GAVE GREAT WISDOM AND BLESSING HELP TO YOUNG PEOPLE
(AND EVEN OLDER PEOPLE, TOO) ABOUT HOW
TO REMEMBER WHAT AND WHERE AND WHO
TO REMEMBER TO BE HAPPY
A Gift (Forever) from Da Kalki
(The World-Teacher, Heart-Master Da Love-Ananda),
as told by Kanya Remembrance, Brahmacharini Shawnee Free Jones,
and their friends.

A moving account of a young girl's confrontation with the real demands of sacred practice, and how Heart-Master Da lovingly Instructed and Served her in her transition through a crisis of commitment to practice that every devotee must, at some point, endure.
$14.95 paper

VEGETABLE SURRENDER,
OR HAPPINESS IS NOT BLUE
by Heart-Master Da and two little girls

The humorous tale of Onion One-Yin and his vegetable friends, who embark on a search for someone who can teach them about happiness and love, and end up learning a great lesson about seeking. Beautifully illustrated with original line drawings.
$12.95 cloth, oversize

THE RENUNCIATION OF CHILDHOOD
AND ADOLESCENCE

Compiled from Heart-Master Da's heretofore unpublished Instructions, this book comprehensively addresses the conscious education of young people in their teenage years. *The Renunciation of Childhood and Adolescence* provides for the modern age an Enlightened vision of the ancient principle of "brahmacharya", or the conscious choice made in one's youth to practice life as a sacred ordeal, devoted to the Realization of the Transcendental and inherently Spiritual Divine Reality.
(forthcoming, mid-1990)
$14.95 paper

LOOK AT THE SUNLIGHT ON THE WATER
EDUCATING CHILDREN FOR A LIFE OF
SELF-TRANSCENDING LOVE AND HAPPINESS:
AN INTRODUCTION

Full of eminently practical guidance for the "whole bodily" and sacred education of children and young people, this simple, straightforward, informative text is also perhaps the best available brief summation of Heart-Master Da Love-Ananda's Wisdom-Teaching on the first three stages of life, or the period from infancy to adulthood.
New Standard Edition (forthcoming, late 1991)
$12.95 paper

AUDIO-VISUAL PUBLICATIONS

VIDEOTAPES

THE WAY OF THE HEART
An Introduction to the "Radical" Teaching and Blessing Work
of the Western-Born Adept, Da Kalki
(The World-Teacher, Heart-Master Da Love-Ananda)

Incorporating rare segments of recent and historical footage, Part One tells the Story of Heart-Master Da Love-Ananda's Divine Birth, the Ordeal of Transformation He underwent to prepare Himself as an Agent of Awakening for others, and the "radical" Purity of His Teaching Message. Recounting the Sacrificial Process whereby Heart-Master Da fully and perfectly Incarnated as the One Living Divine Consciousness, Part One celebrates the Emergence of His Work of World Blessing.

Part Two (which includes talk excerpts by Heart-Master Da and testimonials by long-time practitioners) describes the Gifts and forms of practice that are Given to all who formally enter into a committed sacred relationship with Heart-Master Da in the traditional manner of Sat-Guru devotion.

Part Three introduces the sacred culture of the Way of the Heart.
$29.95, 2 hours, VHS, NTSC, or PAL format

The Way of the Heart is also available in a modified form, which includes recent footage of Heart-Master Da in Darshan with devotees and other material not included in the full-length version. A brief, summary audiovisual introduction to His Life and Divine Work as the World-Teacher in a world addicted to egoic suffering and seeking.
$19.95, 76 minutes, VHS, NTSC, or PAL format

PERIODICAL

THE FREE DAIST

(The bimonthly religious journal of The Free Daist Communion)

The Free Daist celebrates and chronicles the Appearance of Free Daism, the eternal, ancient, and new religion of God-Realization, as Given in Heart-Master Da Love-Ananda's original, consummate, and unprecedented Revelation of the Way of the Heart.

Subscriptions are US$48.00 per year for six issues. Please send your check or money order (payable to The Dawn Horse Press) to:

The Free Daist
P.O. Box 3680
Clearlake, CA 95422
USA

ORDERING THE BOOKS AND VIDEOTAPES OF HEART-MASTER DA LOVE-ANANDA

The books and videotapes of Heart-Master Da Love-Ananda are available at local bookstores and by mail from The Dawn Horse Book Depot.

Please write to us at the address below for a complete catalogue of books, study courses, and audio-visual publications on the Way of the Heart and traditional sacred literature.

In the USA please add $1.75 for the first book or videotape and $.75 for each additional book or videotape. California residents add 6% sales tax.

Outside the USA please add $4.00 for the first book or videotape and $1.00 for each additional book or videotape.

To order the books and videotapes listed above, and to receive your copy of The Dawn Horse Book Depot Catalogue, please write:

THE DAWN HORSE BOOK DEPOT
P.O. Box 3680
Clearlake, CA 95422, USA
(707) 928-4936

INDEX

A

Adepts, Wisdom and Blessing made
possible through, 14-15, 22
Agency, 214. *See also* Agents; Instrumentality
Agents, 188, 214. *See also* Instruments
ajna chakra, 129
defined, 209
Allison, 80-81
arati
defined, 209
See also Sat-Guru Arati
asana, 119
defined, 208
ash, sacred, 156
Ashram, 202. *See also* Hermitage Ashrams
Ashram Dharma, 126, 208
Atelaite, 126
attention, discipline of, 87
Avadhoot, avadhoota, 47, 174
Avatar, 6-7
Awareness, of an Enlightened person,
117-18

B

Baptized Each One, 159
Basket of Tolerance, The, 131
described, 209
bas mitzvah, 149
defined, 211
Blessing Work (of Heart-Master Da
Love-Ananda), 67-69, 206
the method of the "kiss", 67
Brahmacharini Io. *See* Io, Brahmacharini
Brahmacharini Naamleela. *See* Naamleela, Brahmacharini
Brahmacharinis
balanced and Happy children, 75
the brahmacharya vow, 157, 160
ceremony of re-affirmation, 154,
157, 158-60
daily schedule, 41-42, 75, 79, 92-96
formal initiation as, 76-78

given the name "Free Jones", 156, 158
as potential Instruments and Agents,
187-88
practice of devotion, self-discipline,
service, and meditation, 41, 103-11
signing their vows, 160
their formal uniforms, 156-57, 158-59
their Statement of Intention, 159
their unique background, 74-75
their Upanayana initiation, 76-78
wearing the tilak, 156, 158, 159
See also Hridaya Da Gurukula Brahmacharini Mandala, The
Brahmacharini Shawnee. *See* Shawnee,
Brahmacharini
Brahmacharini Tamarind. *See*
Tamarind, Brahmacharini
brahmacharya, 14, 35-37, 76-77
traditional training, 35, 37, 76, 88, 187
See also brahmacharya discipline (in
the Way of the Heart); brahmacharya practice (in the Way
of the Heart)
brahmacharya discipline (in the Way of
the Heart), 79, 86-88, 92-96,
121-22
appropriate consequences, 92, 99-100
circumstance required to maintain,
85, 93-96, 194-95
daily schedule, 41-42, 75, 79, 92-96
Da-Stick reminders, 119-20, 121, 134
food discipline, 121, 146
The (Free Daist) Lay Brahmacharya
Order, 193-96
See also brahmacharya practice (in
the Way of the Heart); discipline
(in the Way of the heart)
Brahmacharya Order, 35, 37, 193-97
establishment of, 76-78
See also Hridaya Da Gurukula Brahmacharini Mandala, The; Lay
Brahmacharya Order, The (Free
Daist)
brahmacharya practice (in the Way of
the Heart), 37-38, 193-96. *See
also* brahmacharya discipline (in
the Way of the Heart)

"Bright", the, 50, 51-56, 58
"Bubba Free John", 63. *See also* Da
   Kalki (The World-Teacher,
   Heart-Master Da Love-Ananda)
Buddha, 6
bure, 90

C

capitalization, unusual use of, 16-17
celebrations (of The Free Daist Communion), 85-86
   Celebration of the Raising of the
      Giving Tree, 118, 208
   The Feast of God in Every Body,
      134, 210
   The Feast of the Love-Ananda
      Leela, 208, 210
   The Feast of Water and Fire, 195
   The Love of the God-Man Celebra-
      tion, 142, 210
   Naitauba Padavara, 80
celibacy, 195
celibate renunciation, 195-96
character types, 208
children
   devotional practices appropriate for,
      42
   meditative exercise for, 42, 203
   "parenting" of, 77
   plight of contemporary, 13-14
   raising, 14
   Spiritual instruction of, 42
   and the Way of the Heart, 104,
      110-11, 203
Chogyam Trungpa. *See* Trungpa,
   Chogyam
Ciqomi, Halloween at, 89-90
Closser, Lynne, 81-82
conch, 117
   defined, 207
   use at Sri Love-Anandashram, 207
confession, Brahmacharini
   Shawnee's, 101-2
conscious exercise, 41
   defined, 202
"consideration", 76
   defined, 205-6

D

"Da" (Divine Name), 36, 65
Da Kalki (The World-Teacher, Heart-
   Master Da Love-Ananda)
   as a baby, 48-50
   as Brahmacharya Master, 84
   and the "Bright", 51-56, 58
   as the "Bright" Divine Being, 50
   as "Bubba Free John", 63
   childhood experiences, 45-47, 51-53
   at Columbia College, 54
   as "Da Free John", 65
   Darshan of, 23, 114, 173-84
   discovery of "Narcissus", 55
   experience of the death of "Narcis-
      sus", 57-58
   experience of "Samadhi", 59
   as "Franklin Jones", 50-54
   as a "God-Born" Adept, 46
   guidance and Blessings from Swami
      Nityananda, 59-60
   the guiding purpose of His life, 47
   His Awareness, 117-18
   His "Beauty Foot", 27
   His Blessing Work, 67-69, 206
   His Divine Agency, 213
   His Divine Emergence, 65-69, 206
   His first Gift, 42
   His gourd hat, 149, 182
   His Gurukula, 33, 38
   His Heroic Way of Teaching, 62-63
   His Love for children, 24-26
   His Names, 47-48, 65, 207
   His Offering of Satsang, 199-200
   His Offering of Spiritual Help, 15
   His perception of ordinary things,
      117-18
   His "Power Foot", 27
   His Seven Gifts of Grace, 211
   His Spiritual Instruments and Agents,
      214
   His Spiritual Transmission, 106, 111,
      212-13
      defined, 206-7
   His Teaching Work, 63-65
   as Hridaya-Samartha Sat-Guru, 188
   as a legal renunciate, 215
   meditating others, 63
   as Parama Guru of His lineage, 62

Da Kalki *(continued)*
    practice of witnessing and writing, 55
    Re-Awakening in the Vedanta Tem-
        ple, 61-62
    receives the Blessing of Rang Avad-
        hoot, 59
    relationship with the Goddess, 60-62
    response of young devotees to, 22-23
    and Robert the cat, 56
    at Stanford University, 54
    as a student of Rudi (Swami
        Rudrananda), 56-58, 60, 209
    as a student of Swami Muktananda,
        58-59, 60, 208
    tapioca pudding story, 130, 209
    teenage experiences, 53-54
    Who He Is, 6-7
Da Love-Ananda, Heart-Master. *See* Da
    Kalki (The World-Teacher,
    Heart-Master Da Love-Ananda)
dana, 38
Da Namaskar, 207. *See also* Surya
    Namaskar
Dardzinski, Elizabeth, 126
Darshan (of Heart-Master Da Love-
    Ananda), 23, 114
    the Darshan at Taken To Heart,
        173-84
Da-Stick reminders, 119-20, 121, 134
Dau Loloma, 90. *See also* Da Kalki
    (The World-Teacher, Heart-
    Master Da Love-Ananda)
DeLollis, Michelle, letter to Heart-Master
    Da, 22-23
dietary discipline, 83-84, 110, 121. *See
    also* discipline (in the Way of
    the Heart)
discipline (in the Way of the Heart),
    27, 109-10
    of attention, 87
    brahmacharya, 41-42, 79, 86-88, 92-
        96, 121-22
    for children, 27-28
    Da-Stick reminders, 119-20, 121,
        134
    dietary, 83-84, 110, 121
    voluntarily and progressively adopt-
        ed, 4
    See also brahmacharya discipline (in
        the Way of the Heart); Seven
        Gifts of Grace

Divine Emergence of Heart-Master Da
    Love-Ananda, 65-69, 206

E

equanimity, 163
"etheric" dimension, 203

F

Feast of God in Every Body, The, 134
    described, 210
    See also Feast of the Love-Ananda
        Leela, The
Feast of the Love-Ananda Leela, The,
    208
    described, 210
    See also Feast of God in Every
        Body, The
Feast of Water and Fire, The, 195
feeling-Contemplation (of Heart-Master
    Da Love-Ananda), 24, 26,
    106, 109, 205
    the foundation of all practice in the
        Way of the Heart, 207
    See also Way of the Heart, the
"Force", the, 57, 60
fourth stage error, 133. *See also* stages
    of life
Free Daist Brahmacharya School, The,
    196. *See also* Lay Brahmacharya
    Order, The (Free Daist)
Free Daist Communion, The, 200
    formal Friend of, 212
(Free Daist) Lay Brahmacharya Order,
    The. *See* Lay Brahmacharya
    Order, The (Free Daist)
"Free Jones" (name), 156, 157, 158.
    See also Brahmacharinis

G

Giver Of Joy, The, 82
Giving Coat, The, 114, 138
    described, 207
Giving Tree, 118, 208
Goddess, 60-62. *See also* Shakti
Goodall, Jane, 30-31

"Great Woman". *See* Shakti
Guru-devotee relationship, in the Way
    of the Heart, 215
Gurukula, 33
Guru-Seva. *See* Sat-Guru-Seva

H

habits, obsessive, 164-66
Halloween, 85-86, 88, 206
    at Ciqomi, 89-90
Happiness
    cannot be found by seeking, 74,
        104-5
    Feeling of, 19-20
    practice of, 28-29
    term used with children, 104
    the way to be Happy, 109-10
Heart-Master
    accepting guidance and Help from,
        29
    See also Sat-Guru
Heart-Master Da Love-Ananda. *See* Da
    Kalki (The World-Teacher,
    Heart-Master Da Love-Ananda)
Hermitage Ashrams, 24, 74-75
    as Agency and Instrumentality, 214
    defined, 202
    form of life lived at, 75
    of Heart-Master Da Love-Ananda, 202
    See also Naitauba; Sri Love-
        Anandashram
Hermitage Day, 80, 82
Hildegard of Bingen, 31
Holy places, 74-75
honey incident, 80-82, 86
    Brahmacharinis' discipline in
        response to, 84, 86
hridaya, 36. *See also* hridayam
Hridaya Da Gurukula Brahmacharini
    Mandala, The, 36, 154-56, 158,
        189, 193
    the sacred emblem of, 154
    the signs of, 157
    See also Brahmacharinis; Brah-
        macharya Order; Lay Brah-
        macharya Order, The (Free Daist)
Hridaya Da Gurukula Kanyadana
    Kumari Mandala, The, 38-39,
        188-89

as living links to Heart-Master Da
    Love-Ananda, 188
as Spiritual guides for the Brah-
    macharinis, 77-78, 189
hridayam, 47-48. *See also* hridaya
Hridaya-Samartha Sat-Guru, 48, 188.
    See also Sat-Guru
Hridaya-Siddha, 210. *See also* Siddha
Hughes, Jeff, 80-81

I

Indefinable, 174, 182
Instrumentality, 214. *See also* Agency;
    Instruments
Instruments, 187-88, 214. *See also*
    Agents
Io, Brahmacharini, 41, 74
    biting her nails, 150
    the bread hat, 149
    getting the food discipline, 146-47
    her confession to Lynne, 147
    Instructions from Heart-Master Da
        Love-Ananda, 148-49

J

Jagad-Guru, 48
Jesus of Nazareth, 6
Jones, Dorothy (mother of Heart-Master
    Da Love-Ananda), 51
Jones, Frank (father of Heart-Master
    Da Love-Ananda), 51
"Jones, Franklin", 50-54
    Heart-Master Da's assumption of
        the identity of, 50
    See also Da Kalki (The World-
        Teacher, Heart-Master Da Love-
        Ananda)
Jones, Joanne (sister of Heart-Master
    Da Love-Ananda), 51

K

Kachina dolls, traditional gift of, 40
Kalki, 7. *See also* Da Kalki (The
    World-Teacher, Heart-Master
    Da Love-Ananda

kanya, 38
Kanyadana Kumaris. *See* Hridaya Da
    Gurukula Kanyadana Kumari
    Mandala, The
Kanya Navaneeta. *See* Navaneeta, Kanya
Kanya Remembrance, *See* Remem-
    brance, Kanya
Kanya Suprithi. *See* Suprithi, Kanya
Kanya Tripura. *See* Tripura Rahasya,
    Kanya
Kladnik, Sandra, 112-14
Krishna, 7
kumari, 38
kum-kum powder, 156

L

lali drum, 175
Lay Brahmacharya Order, The (Free
    Daist), 193-96
  acceptance into, 196
  adult members, 195
  and emotional-sexual intimacy, 194,
    195
  lifetime vow of practice, 194
  preparation required of young
    applicants, 194-95
  See also brahmacharya discipline (in
    the Way of the Heart); Brah-
    macharya Order; brahmacharya
    practice (in the Way of the
    Heart)
Leela, 129
  defined, 209
leela, 209
letters from Brahmacharini Shawnee
    to Heart-Master Da Love-
    Ananda, 23, 117, 124-38
Long Beach, 128
Look at the Sunlight on the Water, 162-
    63
Love-Ananda, 47
  Name explained, 207
  See also Da Kalki (The World-
    Teacher, Heart-Master Da Love-
    Ananda)
Love-Ananda Gita, The, 108, 124
  described, 207
Love of the God-Man Celebration,
    The, 142

  Brahmacharini Shawnee's experi-
    ence at, 177-79, 182
  described, 210
  lowercase letters, unusual use of, 16-17

M

mackerel incident, 97-100
mala, 78
  defined, 206
mandala, 36
Marpa the Translator, 31
"Ma". *See* Goddess
"Master bead", 206. *See also* mala
Matrix, The, 134
  described, 210
meditation (in the Way of the Heart),
    110, 205. *See also* feeling-
    Contemplation (of Heart-Master
    Da Love-Ananda)
Mother Shakti. *See* Goddess; Shakti
Mountain Of Attention Sanctuary, The,
    74, 167, 202. *See also* Her-
    mitage Ashrams
Muktananda, Swami, 58-58, 126, 208
Mystery, the, 103-5, 140-41, 162-63, 203
Mystics
  fifth stage, 204
  See also stages of life

N

Naamleela, Brahmacharini, 41, 74
  the lesson of the desserts, 162
Naitauba, 47
Naitauba Padavara, 80. *See also* Her-
    mitage Day
"Narcissus", 55-56, 63-64, 208
Navaneeta, Kanya, 164
  her call to all to respond to Heart-
    Master Da Love-Ananda's Great
    Heart-Offering, 190
Neem, roaring like a lion with his
    Heart-Master, 29-30
Nityananda, Swami, 58, 59-60
No Doubt Of God, 97, 99
Notes (from Heart-Master Da Love-
    Ananda), 206

O

Old Testament, story of Samuel, 31
"Open Eyes", 204-5
Ordeal Bath Lodge, 168
Owl Sandwiches, 158

P

Patterson, Laurel, 136
"peculiar" type, 123
 defined, 208
perception, of an Enlightened person, 117-18
Prakashananda, Swami, 95, 206
Prasad, 174
 defined, 211
puja, 116

R

Raising of the Giving Tree, Celebration of the, 118, 208
Ralph Royce, 174
Ramakrishna, 61
Rang Avadhoot, 59
Rato Khyongla Nawang Losang of Dayab, 31-32
reception-release, 137
 defined, 210
Remembrance, Kanya, 39, 73-74, 82, 125
 her meditation, 139-40
 her prayer for Brahmacharini Shawnee, 144-45
renunciation
 celibate, 195-96
 legal, 215
Robert the cat, 56, 65
Rudi. *See* Rudrananda, Swami
Rudrananda, Swami, 56-58, 208
 and the "Force", 57

S

sacramental worship, 116
Sacred Treasures (of the Way of the Heart), 213

Saint John of the Cross, 128
Saints
 fourth stage, 204
 See also stages of life
St. Therese of Lisieux, 133
Samadhi, 59
Samartha Sat-Guru, 48. *See also* Sat-Guru
Samuel, *Old Testament* story of, 31
Sanctuaries. *See* Hermitage Ashrams
saris, 156
Sat-Guru, 48
 accepting guidance and Help from, 29
 See also Heart-Master
Sat-Guru Arati, 132, 209
Sat-Guru-Seva, 133
 defined, 210
 See also service (in the Way of the Heart); Seven Gifts of Grace
Satsang, 160, 169
 defined, 211
 Way of, 199-200
 See also Way of the Heart, the
self-contraction, 105-6
self-discipline. *See* discipline (in the Way of the Heart)
service (in the Way of the Heart), 109, 210. *See also* Sat-Guru-Seva
seva, 210. *See also* Sat-Guru-Seva
Seven Gifts of Grace, 144
 described, 211
 See also Way of the Heart, the
Seven Great Gifts. *See* Seven Gifts of Grace
seven stages of life. *See* stages of life
Shakti, 58, 60-62. *See also* "Bright", the
Shawnee, Brahmacharini, 22, 41, 74
 the bucket-full-of-water hat, 149
 circumstances of her birth, 33
 creating conflicts with the other Brahmacharinis, 91-92
 Darshan experience in 1984, 177-79, 182
 Darshan experience at Taken To Heart, 175-84
 feeling the Mystery, 142, 144
 Heart-Master Da's response to her confession, 103-11
 her confession, 101-2
 her "exile" from the Brahmacharya Order, 99-100

Shawnee, Brahmacharini *(continued)*
  her gratitude for the brahmacharya
    discipline, 169
  her prayer to Heart-Master Da Love-
    Ananda, 145
  her reintegration into the Brah-
    macharya Order, 120-21, 144
  her secret life, 93
  her stay in the village, 112-20, 123-
    38
  her Upanayana initiation, 78
  the honey incident, 80-82
  letters to Heart-Master Da Love-
    Ananda, 23, 117, 124-38
  the mackerel incident, 97-100
  swimming underwater, 168-69
  visits from Kanya Remembrance,
    112-13, 116-17, 119
Shiny, 123. *See also* Shawnee, Brahmacharini
Siddha, 133
  defined, 210
siddhis, 118
"solid" type, 208
Spiritual Cannibalism, 126, 128, 133,
  209
Sri Love-Anandashram, 48, 74, 202.
    See also Hermitage Ashrams;
    Naitauba
stages of life
  first three, 203-4
  first, 203
  second, 103, 203
  third, 103, 148-49, 203-4
  last four stages, 204-5
  fourth, 204
    fourth stage error, 133, 204
  fifth, 204
  sixth, 204
  seventh, 204-5
  stages described, 203-5
Story Sabatino, 80-81
student-beginner, prepared, 194, 195.
    See also Way of the Heart, the
Suprithi, Kanya, 118, 129
  her praise for the Gift of practice,
    188-89
Surya Namaskar, 113, 127
  defined, 207

Swami Muktananda. *See* Muktananda,
  Swami
Swami Nityananda. *See* Nityananda,
  Swami
Swami Prakashananda. *See*
  Prakashananda, Swami
Swami Rudrananda. *See* Rudrananda,
  Swami

T

Taken To Heart, the Darshan at, 173-
  84
Tamarind, Brahmacharini, 41, 74
  the Gift of the Kachina doll, 40
  her idiosyncrasy, 164-66
  Instruction from Heart-Master Da
    Love-Ananda, 165
tapas, 91. *See also* discipline (in the
  Way of the Heart)
tapioca pudding story, 130, 209
"Tcha", 119
  defined, 208
Teaching Word (of Heart-Master Da
    Love-Ananda)
  as Agency and Instrumentality, 214
  perpetual copyright to, 212-13
Teaching Work (of Heart-Master Da
    Love-Ananda), 63-65
  completion of, 65-67
  a Gift of His Grace, 211
  His Heroic Way of Teaching, 63-64
third eye, 209
tilak, 156
Tripura Rahasya, Kanya, 125
  her description of how Heart-Master
    Da Love-Ananda's Grace Flows
    to all, 189-90
Trungpa, Chogyam, 32-33
tulkus, 31-33, 88, 95
  training of, 32-33
Tumomama Sanctuary, 74, 162, 202.
    See also Hermitage Ashrams
Turtle Cove, 149, 182
Two Secrets (yours, and Mine), The, 7,
  138, 189

U

Upanayana ceremony, 76-78, 145. *See also* Brahmacharinis

V

Vedanta Temple, 61-62
Vishnu, Avatars of, 6-7
vision quest
    of the American Indian, 34
    in the Way of the Heart, 34-35, 41
"vital-physical" dimension, 203
"vital" type, 208
vows, brahmacharya, 157, 160. *See also* Brahmacharinis

W

Water and Narcissus, 124, 208
Way of the Heart, the
    brahmacharya practice in, 193-96
    a Call to become responsible for oneself, 212
    for children, 104, 110-11, 203
    the foundation practice, 207
    the Guru-devotee relationship in, 215
    the Offering of Satsang, 199-200
    practice characterized by equanimity, 163
    sadhana of, 106-11
    Seven Gifts of Grace, 211
    student-beginner, prepared, 194, 195
    the Wisdom-Teaching of, 213
    See also feeling-Contemplation (of Heart-Master Da Love-Ananda); Satsang
What and Where and Who To Remember To Be Happy: A Simple Explanation Of The Way Of The Heart (For Children, and Everyone Else), 20-21, 140-41, 203
will, development of, 203-4
World-Teacher, 48
World-Teacher, Heart-Master Da Love-Ananda, The. *See* Da Kalki (The World-Teacher, Heart-Master Da Love-Ananda)

Y

Yogis
    fifth stage, 204
    See also stages of life

For more information about forms of involvement
in the Way of the Heart Revealed by
Da Kalki
(The World-Teacher,
Heart-Master Da Love-Ananda),
please write to us at the address below:

Correspondence Department

THE FREE DAIST COMMUNION
P. O. Box 3680
Clearlake, California 95422
USA
Phone: (707) 928-4936